Faith First

Grade Three

Faith First Development Team

RCL

RESOURCES FOR CHRISTIAN LIVING™

"The Ad Hoc Committee to Oversee
the Use of the Catechism,
National Conference of Catholic Bishops,
has found this catechetical series, copyright 2000,
to be in conformity with
the *Catechism of the Catholic Church*."

NIHIL OBSTAT
Rev. Msgr. Glenn D. Gardner, J.C.D.
Censor Librorum

IMPRIMATUR
† Most Rev. Charles V. Grahmann
Bishop of Dallas

March 10, 1999

The Nihil Obstat and Imprimatur are official declarations that
the material reviewed is free of doctrinal or moral error. No
implication is contained therein that those granting the Nihil
Obstat and Imprimatur agree with the contents, opinions, or
statements expressed.

Send all inquiries to:
RCL • Resources for Christian Living
200 East Bethany Drive
Allen, Texas 75002-3804

Toll Free   877-275-4725
Fax   800-688-8356

Visit us at **www.RCLweb.com**
            www.FaithFirst.com

Printed in the United States of America

20303   ISBN 0-7829-0919-1 (Student Book)

20313   ISBN 0-7829-0920-5 (Teacher Guide)

20323   ISBN 0-7829-0921-3 (Catechist Guide)

4 5 6 7 8 9 10
01 02 03 04 05

ACKNOWLEDGMENTS

Scripture excerpts are taken or adapted from the *New
American Bible with Revised New Testament and Psalms*
Copyright © 1991, 1986, 1970 Confraternity of Christian
Doctrine, Washington, DC. Used with permission. All rights
reserved. No part of the *New American Bible* may be
reproduced by any means without the permission of the
copyright owner.

Excerpts are taken or adapted from the English translation
of *The Roman Missal* © 1973, International Committee on
English in the Liturgy, Inc. (ICEL); excerpts from the English
translation of *Rite of Penance* © 1974, ICEL; excerpts from
the English translation of *Rite of Baptism for Children* © 1969,
ICEL; excerpts from the English translation of *Rite of
Confirmation*, second edition © 1975, ICEL; excerpts from
the English translation of *A Book of Prayers* © 1982, ICEL;
excerpts from *Book of Blessings* © 1987, ICEL. All rights
reserved.

Photograph and Art Credits appear on page 336.

Faith First Development Team

Developing a religion program requires the gifts
and talents of many different individuals
working together as a team. RCL is proud
to acknowledge these dedicated people.

Advisory Board

Rev. Louis J. Cameli
Judith Deckers
Rev. Robert D. Duggan
Rev. Virgil Elizondo
Jacquie Jambor
Maureen A. Kelly
Elaine McCarron, SCN
Rev. Frank McNulty
Rev. Ronald J. Nuzzi
Kate Sweeney Ristow

Grade 3 Writers

Student Book	Catechist/Teacher Guides
Mary Beth Jambor	Mary Beth Jambor
Yvette Nelson	Yvette Nelson
Anna Dolores Ready	Anna Dolores Ready

Editorial

Blake Bergen
Patricia A. Classick
Ed DeStefano
Jack Gargiulo
Karen Griffith
Anne Battes Kirby
Keith Ksobiech
Ronald C. Lamping
Joan Lathen
Ed Leach
Marianne K. Lenihan
Myrtle E. Teffeau

Art and Design

Pat Bracken
Andrea Friedman
Kristy Howard
Sheila Lehnert
Karen Malzeke-McDonald
Margaret Matus
Carol-Anne Wilson

Production

Mark Burgdorff
Laura Fremder
Becky Ivey
Jenna Nelson

Executive Board

Maryann Nead   Kim Duty
                    Richard C. Leach

3

Contents

Welcome to Faith First

My name is _____ .

I like to be called _____ .

One of the best things about me is _____

_____ .

This year I hope I learn _____ .

_____

People in My Family

_____
_____
_____
_____
_____
_____
_____
_____

Favorite Things

Holiday _____

Bible story _____

Animal _____

Game _____

Food _____

Sport or hobby _____

A Prayer for the Beginning of Third Grade

Dear God,
I think third grade is going to be great. Thank you for
creating my friends, my family, and me. I am happy that
you are always with me. Help me to show my faith in all
that I do. Thank you for helping me to know you better.

Amen.

Unit 1—We Believe

Parent Page—Unit 1: We Believe

Your Role

Third graders are a unique group and fun to be around. They have acquired many skills—they can read and write; organize their time; help without much supervision; and are still willing to be a part of something new. Friends are certainly important, but most third graders are still content to spend time with parents as well. These are days we as parents will treasure.

In religious education, your third grader is at an age when he or she can grasp more meaning behind the concepts taught. Third graders ask direct questions but are beginning to think less in terms of black and white. They are beginning to see alternatives and options. Your guidance at this stage of moral development is crucial as they move forward in their ability to make their own decisions.

You continue to be the primary educator of your child in the life of faith. This means educating in the broadest sense of the word. By watching you as you live your life, seeing what you do and hearing what you say, your child develops a sense of what is important in life. Children truly do learn what they live. If faith is important in your home, then faith will be important to your child as he or she goes through life.

What We're Teaching

The first unit teaches the students about the creed—what we believe. Topics include how we come to know about God; the beauty of God's creation; Mary and her trust in God; Jesus and the Holy Spirit. You might like to take a look at the scripture lesson in this unit on women of the Bible—Sarah, Ruth, Esther and Hannah. Many of us are unfamiliar with the stories of these women of deep faith. This might be an ideal time to read the Bible with your child. Begin with Hannah and continue through the call of Samuel. Third graders love this story.

Visit our web site at www.FaithFirst.com

What Difference Does It Make?

Third graders are growing in their ability to reach out and help others. Look through the "What Difference Does It Make in My Life" pages in your child's book. See if you feel that your child has understood the concept, and then look for ways to reinforce the learning throughout the week. In this unit, you may wish to pay special attention to page 57 which challenges your child to put the gospel message into action. Help your child see what he or she can do in your home and with friends. Encourage your child to do acts of kindness, generosity, and patience in small daily things. You might even have a "Be Kind" day when everyone in your house has to go out of their way to help everyone else. These are the things that help bring the gospel message to life for your child.

Unit Opener Photographs: (top left) statue of the Risen Christ; (top right) stained-glass window of Saint Paul; (bottom) dolphin and the sea—gifts of God's creation.

God Speaks to Us

We Pray

Glory to the Father,
and to the Son,
and to the
Holy Spirit:
as it was in the
beginning, is now,
and will be for ever.
Amen.

God is always
telling us who he is.
God reveals himself
to us as one God in
three Persons. What
do you already know
about God?

*This stained-glass
window reminds us
of our belief that there
is one God in three
Persons: Father, Son,
and Holy Spirit.*

A new school year can be filled with excitement. Making new friends and getting to know old friends better are wonderful parts of being in third grade. God is always inviting us to get to know him better too. What are some of the ways you think you will learn more about God this year?

Faith Focus

What do we mean by the Holy Trinity?

Faith Vocabulary

Holy Trinity

The Holy Trinity is the belief that there is one God in three Persons: God the Father, God the Son, and God the Holy Spirit.

creed

A creed is a prayer that tells what we believe.

The Holy Trinity

In order to know God it is important for us to know what we mean by the mystery of the **Holy Trinity.** When we believe in the Holy Trinity, we believe that there is one God in three Persons. The three Persons are God the Father, God the Son, and God the Holy Spirit. This is a mystery because we cannot fully understand it.

God the Father is our Creator. God the Son is Jesus Christ. God the Holy Spirit is our helper. Each Person of the Trinity helps us live as God's children. God created us to share in his love forever.

We Pray the Creed

We have a special prayer, or **creed**, that we say each Sunday at Mass. It is called the Nicene Creed. When we pray this prayer, we say that we believe in the Holy Trinity.

We believe in one God,
the Father, the Almighty,
maker of heaven and earth.

We believe in one Lord, Jesus Christ,
the only Son of God.

We believe in the Holy Spirit,
the Lord, the giver of life.

To Help You Remember

1. Who are the three Persons of the Holy Trinity?

2. In the Nicene Creed what do we say we believe about God?

Picturing the Trinity

Saint Patrick used a shamrock to teach people about the Trinity. On the shamrock's leaves, write the names of the three Persons of the Holy Trinity. On the stem write the name we use when we speak of one God in three Persons.

On the lines write one thing you can do today to show that you believe in God.

_____

_____

11

Faith Vocabulary

Sacred Scriptures
The Sacred Scriptures
are the written word of
God. The Sacred
Scriptures are also
called the Bible.

Old Testament
The first part of the
Bible, which tells the
story of God's people
who lived before Jesus
was born, is called the
Old Testament.

New Testament
The second part of the
Bible, which tells about
Jesus and the early
Church, is called the
New Testament.

One way we learn about people is by
reading stories about them. One way we
learn about God is by reading the Bible
and listening to it read aloud at Mass.

God Speaks to Us in the Bible

We believe the Bible is the written
word of God. The Bible is also called the
Sacred Scriptures. The words *sacred
scriptures* mean "holy writings." The Holy
Spirit helped God's people to write the
Sacred Scriptures.

God speaks to us in the writings in the
Bible. In the Bible we learn that God is holy.
This means that God is all-good. We also
learn that God is everlasting because he
had no beginning and will have no end.

The Bible has two parts, the **Old
Testament** and the **New Testament.** The
Old Testament tells us about God and the
Israelite people God chose as his own
special people. In this part of the Bible,
we learn about God's people who lived
before Jesus.

The Bible especially tells us that our God is a God who keeps his promises. We learn this from reading the stories of Noah, Abraham, Moses, and the prophets. Prophets were people who reminded God's people about God's promises to them.

The New Testament is the second part of the Bible. It tells us about Jesus and his followers. In the New Testament is a letter that the apostle Paul wrote to Timothy. In it Paul reminds Timothy of what we can learn from the Bible.

Always remember that the holy writings come to us from God. The Bible can help you and all people to do good works in the name of Jesus, God's Son.

Based on 2 Timothy 3:14–16

To Help You Remember

1. What are the two main parts of the Bible?

2. What do we learn about God from the Bible?

With My Family

Read a story in the Bible. Act out the story for your family.

Jesus shows us that we can always trust God. God is always faithful to his promises to us.

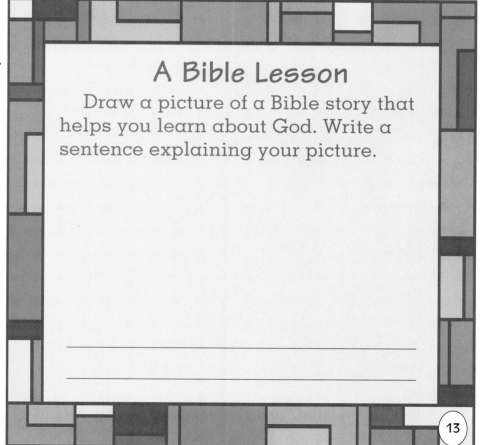

A Bible Lesson

Draw a picture of a Bible story that helps you learn about God. Write a sentence explaining your picture.

Faith Vocabulary

People of God
The People of God is a name we give to the Church.

Christians
People who are baptized and believe in Jesus Christ are called Christians.

We have learned that God speaks to us through the Bible. God also reveals himself to us, or tells us about himself, through all creation but especially through people.

God Speaks to Us Through the Church Community

During his life on earth, Jesus called people to follow him. These followers became the first members of the Church.

Jesus also chose the apostles to be the leaders of the Church. Jesus knew that the community of his followers, the Church, would need strong leaders. They would help the other followers live as he taught them.

The Bible tells us about the apostles and the first members of the Church.

Many people came to believe in Jesus. They listened to the teachings of the apostles. They cared for one another. They sold their belongings and shared their money.

They prayed together. They broke bread together. Together they joyfully praised God.

Based on Acts of the Apostles 2:42–47

We believe that the Church is the **People of God.** All people who are baptized are called **Christians.** Christians follow Jesus as their teacher. Jesus is the head of the Church. The Holy Spirit helps the Church grow.

We belong to the Catholic Church. Catholics pray and celebrate together in a parish. We work and pray with members of our parish family. We learn about God. We do the things Jesus taught us to do.

To Help You Remember

1. How did the first followers of Jesus live?

2. In what ways does the Church help us know and understand God?

Learning from the People of God

Think about the people in your parish. Draw or write some of the ways your parish family teaches you about God.

God reveals himself as the Holy Trinity. The Holy Trinity is our belief that there is one God in three Persons: God the Father, God the Son, and God the Holy Spirit. God tells us who he is through the Bible and through the church community.

Seeing Is Believing

Since the time of the early Church, Christians have expressed their love for God through beautiful artwork. Stained glass, paintings, and mosaics are some of the ways that artists have shown their belief in God.

What does each of these pictures tell you about God?

You come to know God through people. The people in your church community show you who God is. The people in your family also help you come to know God.

I LOVE YOU

Your family teaches you about God through their words and actions. And every day you help your family know God better too. Write what you can say and do that helps your family members know God better.

This is how I show my family who God is.

Words: _____

_____

Actions: _____

_____

THANKS FOR HELPING

My Faith Choice

This week I will help my family to know God better by

_____

_____ .

And now we pray.

We believe in one God—God the Father, God the Son, God the Holy Spirit.
Based on Nicene Creed

Use a word in the box to complete each sentence.

Bible	**New Testament**
Christians	**Church** **Trinity**

1. The _____ is the written word of God.

2. _____ are baptized followers of Jesus Christ.

3. The _____ is the People of God.

4. God as Father, Son, and Holy Spirit is the Holy _____ .

5. The _____ tells us about Jesus and the early Church.

Fill in the blanks.

1. The three Persons in one God are God the _____ , God the _____ , and God the _____ .

2. The prayer we pray at Mass that tells that we believe in the Trinity is the _____ .

3. Jesus chose the _____ to be leaders of the Church.

Think and share with your family.
Name one way your family honors God as Father, Son, and Holy Spirit.

Visit our web site at www.FaithFirst.com

The Beauty of God's Creation

We Pray

How numerous are
    your works, O LORD!
In wisdom you have
    formed them all—
the earth is full of
    your creatures.
Bless the LORD,
    O my soul!

Based on Psalm 104:24

God's beautiful creation tells us about God. Name three things God created. How do they show God's goodness?

The world is filled with God's wonderful gifts of creation.

Faith Focus

What does the beauty of creation tell us about God?

Faith Vocabulary

creation

All that God has made is known as creation.

Picture in your mind the sun, moon, and stars, beautiful plants, interesting animals, and wonderful people. What do all these things have in common?

If you said they are all part of God's **creation,** you are right. What are some other gifts of creation?

A Loving Creator

God our Father created everything and everyone out of love. All that God created is good.

God is with us at every moment. God cares for all that he has made. Through our eyes and other senses we can come to know God's beauty in the beauty of creation.

The Story of Creation

The very first book in the Old Testament tells the story of creation.

God made light for day and darkness for night. God made the earth and sky and sea. God filled the earth with plants.

God made the sun and the moon and stars. God saw that it was good.

God made birds for the sky and fish for the water. God saw that it was good.

God made animals for the land. God saw that it was good.

Based on Genesis 1:1–25, 31

Our five senses help us to appreciate all the wonderful things God has made. Think about the gifts of creation that you can see, hear, smell, taste, and touch. Creation helps us know God's love for us.

To Help You Remember

1. Who created the universe?

2. How can the beauty of creation help us to know God?

Sensing God in Creation

Complete the sentences with your favorite examples of God's beautiful creation.

My favorite part of creation **to look at** is _____.

My favorite part of creation **to listen to** is _____.

My favorite part of creation **to smell** is _____.

My favorite part of creation **to touch** is _____.

My favorite part of creation **to taste** is _____.

Faith Focus

In whose image did God create human beings?

Faith Vocabulary

Genesis
The Book of Genesis is the first book of the Bible.

God Created People

Did you know that you are unique? That means there is no one else quite like you. God created every person as a unique and special individual. We each have our own likes and dislikes. We each have our own talents and abilities.

God created each of us in his own image. He created us with a spiritual soul. Our soul makes us like God. God created us to love him as our loving Father.

God invites us to share our lives with him. God always shares his life and love with us. We belong to God, our creator. We are God's children.

The Book of **Genesis** is the very first book of the Bible. It tells us that God is our creator. We are the most wonderful part of creation.

People were created in God's image. God blessed them. God gave them the world to care for.

God asked the people to care for the fish of the sea. People needed to care for the birds of the air too. God asked the people to care for all living things.

God saw that everything he made was good.

Based on
Genesis 1:26–31

By creating us in his own image, God gives us a wonderful responsibility. God calls us to love and care for his world.

God made everything because God is love. He wants to share his love with us forever.

To Help You Remember

1. In whose image are we created?

2. What does God invite us to do?

In God's Image

God created you and all people in his own image. Draw a picture of yourself. Then tell how you show God's goodness.

Faith Vocabulary

Divine Providence
God's caring love is known as Divine Providence.

Psalms
Songs of prayer and praise to God found in the Bible are called psalms. The Book of Psalms is in the Old Testament.

Jesus taught us that God is always with us to help us live as his children. We do not have to do this alone. He taught people to trust in God's caring love for us.

Divine Providence

We call God's caring love for us his **Divine Providence.** God is our Father and creator. God created us to share in his goodness and love.

Jesus told us how much God cares about us. Jesus said,

"Do not worry about what you will eat or drink. Do not worry about what you will wear.

"Look at the birds in the sky. Your heavenly Father feeds them. Look at the fields of grass. God clothes the fields with beautiful wild flowers.

"Do not worry. Your heavenly Father knows what you need."

Based on Matthew 6:25–32

When we trust in God's caring love for us, we believe that God is always with us. We never have to handle our problems alone.

24

We Praise God

We thank God for all he has created. We give praise to God for his goodness.

The Book of **Psalms** is in the Old Testament. Many of the psalms praise and thank God for his Divine Providence.

The LORD will bless us.
God has given the earth to his
    children.
We will bless the LORD, now and
    forever.

Based on Psalm 115:16, 18

To Help You Remember

1. What do we call God's caring love for us?

2. Why do we praise God?

With My Family

Find pictures that show the beauty of God's creation. As a family share what the pictures tell you about God.

Trusting in God's Care

Every day you trust God to care for you. Complete the prayer by naming some of the ways God helps and protects you.

God, my Creator,

You care for me by _____ and by

_____ . You gave me _____

and _____ to help care for me. I

remember how you helped me when _____

_____. Every day you protect me from

_____ . I thank you and praise you, O God!

God is the Creator. God created the universe and everything and everyone in it. All God created is good.

Creation and Our Parish Church

When we gather together in our parish church, we use God's beautiful creation to help us worship God.

The windows of our church allow the light and warmth of the sun to come inside. Fresh flowers and plants often decorate the altar. Even the candles we light are made from beeswax!

The bread and wine used at Mass come to us from the earth. Sometimes oil is used in our celebrations. The oil comes from olives, one of the many fruits of creation. Water too is often used. It reminds us that God gives us new life in Jesus through Baptism.

God's beautiful creation fills our churches!

Think about your parish church or other churches you have visited. What signs of creation do you see there?

What Difference Does It Make in My Life?

You are made in God's own image. God created you and all human beings and the universe out of love. God asks you to work with other people to help God to care for creation.

God's World Is My World

God's beautiful creation touches your life all the time. Stop and listen. Look and wonder. List the gifts of creation you have discovered in the world around you.

____

____

____

____

How can you care for one of these gifts?

____

____

____

My Faith Choice

This week I will try to take better care of all God's gifts of creation. One gift I will pay extra attention to is __________ __________________________ .

And now we pray.

O LORD, my God,
you are great
indeed!
All the earth is full
of your creatures.
Based on Psalm 104:1, 24

God created everything that is good. Draw a line to connect each word with its meaning.

Words	Meanings
1. creation	a. A song of praise
2. psalm	b. God's loving care for us
3. Creator	c. All that God has made
4. Divine Providence	d. God, who made everything and everyone

Use the words in the box to complete the sentences.

caring	Jesus	love	people	creation

1. The beauty of creation shows God's _____ for us.

2. God created _____ in his own image.

3. _____ told a story about God's Divine Providence.

4. God never stops _____ for all he has created.

5. God asks people to help care for _____ .

Think and share with your family.
Talk with your family about a place where you can see the beauty of God's creation. Then share how the beauty of creation helps your family to know God.

Visit our web site at www.FaithFirst.com

Mary Trusted in God

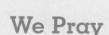

We Pray

Almighty Father, you have shown us the beauty of your power by raising up Mary of Nazareth and making her the mother of our Savior.

Based on the Alternative Opening Prayer for the Feast of the Annunciation, March 25

Mary trusted in God completely. Because of her great trust and faith in God, she is a model of faith for all Christians. How did Mary show her faith and trust in God?

This statue of Mary and Jesus reminds us of Mary's faith in God.

The Faith of Mary

Faith Focus

What did the angel Gabriel announce to Mary?

Faith Vocabulary

Mary
Mary is the mother of Jesus, the Son of God who became like us.

Annunciation
The announcement of Jesus' birth to Mary by the angel Gabriel is called the Annunciation.

faith
Belief and trust in God is called faith.

Stained-glass window of Mary and the angel Gabriel.

With My Family

Make a prayer card. Use Mary's answer to the angel Gabriel. Share your prayer card with your family. Pray this prayer of faith often.

It is always exciting to hear good news. What good news did you hear today?

Mary Says Yes to God

Some of the best news that we will ever hear is that God sent his Son, Jesus, into our world. To announce this good news, God sent the angel Gabriel to **Mary,** a young girl who lived in a town named Nazareth. The Church calls the announcement of Jesus' birth to Mary the **Annunciation.**

Act out what happened next.

ANGEL: "Hail, Mary. The Lord is with you."

MARY: "What do you mean?"

ANGEL: "You shall bear a son and you shall name him Jesus."

MARY: "How can this be?"

ANGEL: "The Holy Spirit will come to you. Your son will be God's own Son."

MARY: "Yes! I will do what God wants me to do."

Based on Luke 1:26–38

Mary believed that God's word would come true. She had great **faith** in God's love for her.

To Help You Remember

1. What message did the angel Gabriel bring to Mary?

2. How did Mary show her trust in God?

Faith and Trust in God

Circle the seven faith terms in the puzzle that tell you something about the Annunciation.

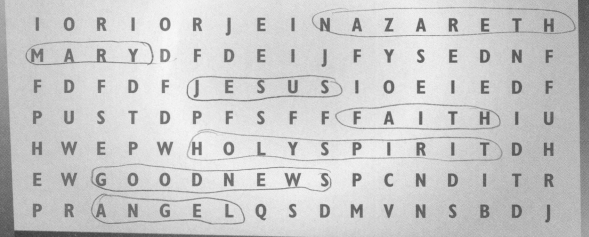

```
I O R I O R J E I N A Z A R E T H
M A R Y D F D E I J F Y S E D N F
F D F D F J E S U S I O E I E D F
P U S T D P F S F F A I T H I U
H W E P W H O L Y S P I R I T D H
E W G O O D N E W S P C N D I T R
P R A N G E L Q S D M V N S B D J
```

Faith Vocabulary

Visitation
The visit that Mary, the mother of Jesus, had with Elizabeth, her relative, is called the Visitation.

canticle
A song of praise to God is called a canticle.

Magnificat
Mary's canticle is called the Magnificat.

Mary Visits Elizabeth

One day when Mary was waiting for Jesus to be born, she went to visit a relative whose name was Elizabeth. She was going to have a baby too. Act out what happened next.

MARY: "Hello, Elizabeth! God be with you!"

ELIZABETH: "Blessed are you, Mary! And blessed is your child that will soon be born. Thank you for saying yes to God. Blessed are you because you trusted God."

MARY: "My soul praises the great goodness of God! My spirit rejoices in God, who is my savior. God has done great things for me! Holy is his name. His promise of mercy to his people has come true."

Based on Luke 1:39–55

Mary's visit to Elizabeth is known as the **Visitation.** When they met, Elizabeth praised Mary because Mary trusted God. Mary shows us how to trust in God's great love for us. She is a model of faith for us.

Mary's Song of Praise

The last words Mary says to Elizabeth in the play you just acted out are a kind of prayer called a **canticle.** Canticles are songs of praise we sing to God for all the wonderful things God has done for us. The Church calls Mary's song of praise the **Magnificat.**

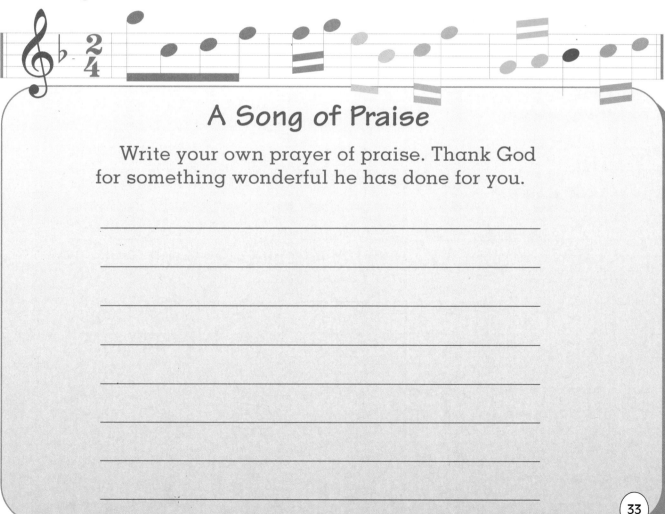

A Song of Praise

Write your own prayer of praise. Thank God for something wonderful he has done for you.

_____

_____

_____

_____

_____

_____

_____

Faith Focus

What happened at the Nativity?

Faith Vocabulary

Joseph
Joseph is the foster father of Jesus and the husband of Mary.

Bethlehem
The town where Jesus was born is called Bethlehem.

Nativity
The birth of Jesus is known as the Nativity.

Mary Gives Birth to Jesus

When Mary was about to have her baby, the ruler of the country that she and Joseph were living in wanted to take a census. This means that the ruler, Caesar Augustus, wanted to count how many people were living there.

Caesar Augustus asked everyone to go to their hometown to be counted. The hometown of **Joseph**, Mary's husband, was **Bethlehem**.

When Mary and Joseph arrived in Bethlehem, people filled the city. They looked, but they could find no inn where they could rest. So they stayed in a place where animals slept and ate.

Jesus was born there. Mary wrapped him in blankets. She laid him in a manger from which the animals ate.

Based on Luke 2:1–7

The Holy Spirit helped Mary believe that God had great plans for her and her son, Jesus. Because of Mary's trust in God, God sent his own Son into the world to save us from sin. The Church calls the birth of Jesus the **Nativity.**

The Bible tells us that after our first parents sinned, God made a promise. He promised to send a savior into the world.

Mary is the woman whom the Bible tells us would give birth to the savior God promised to send. When the time was right according to God's plan, Jesus was born. Jesus, the Son of God, is the Savior of the world.

To Help You Remember

1. Where did Mary and Joseph go to be counted?

2. How did Mary's faith in God help to bring God's Son into the world?

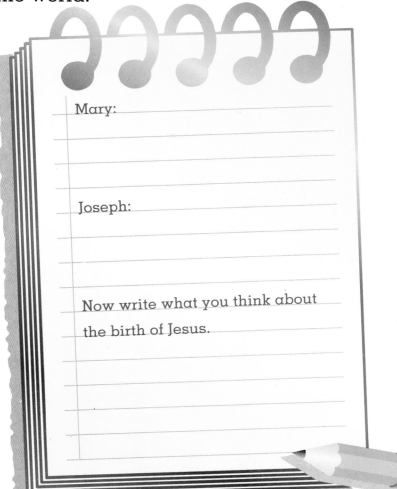

Mary:

Joseph:

Now write what you think about the birth of Jesus.

An Interview with Mary and Joseph

Pretend that you are a news reporter in Bethlehem. You learn about Jesus' birth. Interview Mary and Joseph. Ask them their thoughts about the birth of Jesus.

Catholic Christians honor Mary as our greatest saint. Mary's faith and trust in God help us know how to live as God's children.

We Honor Mary

Catholics show their love and respect for Mary in many ways. We remember her on special days throughout the year. On March 25 we remember and celebrate the Annunciation. We also say special prayers to Mary. We place statues and pictures of Mary in our churches, homes, schools, and hospitals.

These works of art show how Catholics honor Mary, the Mother of God, throughout the world. What do these pictures tell you about Mary?

You can learn so many things from the story of Mary, the mother of Jesus. You can learn about her faith and trust in God. You can learn about helping others. You can learn about prayer in the way Mary praised God.

Saying Yes to God

Mary said yes and trusted God. Design a poster with words and pictures that shows ways you can trust God and say yes to what he asks of you.

My Faith Choice

What is something that God might be asking you to do that you can say yes to this week? This week I will

_____.

And now we pray.

"Hail Mary, full of grace. The Lord is with you. Blessed are you among women."

Draw a line through each ending that does not belong.

1. The Church celebrates the Annunciation because on that day
   - (a.) the angel Gabriel made an announcement to Mary.
   - b. Mary visited Elizabeth.
   - c. Jesus was born.

2. The Church celebrates the Visitation because on that day
   - a. the angel Gabriel made an announcement to Mary.
   - (b.) Mary visited Elizabeth.
   - c. Jesus was born.

3. The Church celebrates the Nativity because on that day
   - a. the angel Gabriel made an announcement to Mary.
   - b. Mary visited Elizabeth.
   - (c.) Jesus was born.

Answer this question.

How did Mary show that she trusted God's love and believed in God?

Mary showed that she trusted God's love and believed in God because

Think and share with your family.

With your family, look up the following Bible verses: Luke 1:35, Luke 1:45, and Luke 2:14. Choose one to memorize. Say it when you say good night to one another each evening.

Visit our web site at www.FaithFirst.com

Women of Faith

A Scripture Story

We Pray

My heart rejoices
in the LORD!
There is no holy one
like the LORD!
He raises the needy
from the dust.
He will guard the
footsteps of his
faith-filled ones.

Based on
1 Samuel 2:1–2, 8–9

We read about
many women of faith
in the Old Testament.
Hannah, a faith-filled
woman, prayed the
prayer above. What
stories have you
heard about women
of faith in the Bible?

The stained-glass
window shows Esther,
another faith-filled
woman of the Old
Testament. Esther, who
became queen of Persia,
was a woman of great
hope and trust in God.

Bible Background

Faith Focus

How did Sarah, Hannah, and Ruth show their faith in God?

Faith Vocabulary

judge
A judge was a leader of God's people before there were kings.

Sarah

Like Mary, Jesus' mother, you believe in God. One important thing you believe is that God loves you. Who helps you to believe in God's love for you? Your mother and father? Your teachers and friends? By their words and actions, they show you God's love. You learn about God from them. Then you believe in God's love even more.

Mary

Women of the Old Testament

Mary learned about God by hearing the stories of her people. She heard stories about women of great faith.

One faith-filled woman of the Old Testament was Sarah. Sarah believed God's promise to her and gave birth to Isaac. He became one of the great leaders of God's people.

Hannah was another woman of great faith. She too prayed to God for a child. Soon Hannah gave birth to Samuel. He became a great **judge** of God's people.

Hannah

Ruth was another faith-filled woman. Trusting God's love, she left her own home and traveled to a new place. There she took care of her husband's mother, Naomi, after both their husbands died. Jesus was a descendant of Ruth.

These women believed in God's love for them. Many years later their example helped Mary. Their example helps us today.

Ruth

To Help You Remember

1. How did God answer the prayers of Sarah and Hannah?

2. What do you think Mary learned from these women of faith?

Your Faith Model

Sarah, Hannah, and Ruth were Mary's ancestors in faith. They are our ancestors in faith too. Think about a woman of faith you know. Then complete these sentences.

The woman of faith I know is _____.

She shows her faith in God by _____

_____.

I can follow her example by _____

_____.

Reading the Word of God

Faith Focus

How did Esther show her faith in God?

Faith Vocabulary

Persia

Persia is the ancient name of a country to the east of the Holy Land.

In Old Testament times, soldiers forced God's people to go to **Persia.** There they lived far from their homeland. Life was sometimes hard for them in Persia. But they trusted God's love and prayed for help. God answered their prayers through a woman named Esther.

Esther's Faith Saves Her People

Esther was a Jewish woman who was made queen of Persia. Soon she learned of a plot to kill her people. Esther prayed to God and said,

"My LORD, you alone are God. Help me, for I am alone and I have no help but you. As a child I learned that you chose my people. I learned that you have kept all your promises to us.

"Now we are being forced to live in another country. People want to kill us. They want us to stop praying to you. O God, remember us here. Show us your love. Save your people from evil. Save us by your power.

"Help me, O God, for I am alone in this palace. I have no one but you. You know I will do all you want.

"Take away my fear. Give me courage. Put good words in my mouth when I speak to the king."

Based on Esther C:14–30

Esther believed that God would protect his people. Fearlessly, she told the king about the plot to kill her people.

The king believed Esther and saved God's people, who were being forced to live in Persia. Because of her faith in God, Esther became a hero to her people.

To Help You Remember

1. Why did Esther ask God for help?

2. How did God answer Esther's prayer?

EXTRA!!! The Times EXTRA!!!

News Flash! News Flash!

Imagine that you are a newspaper reporter. You know about the plot and about Esther and the king of Persia. Write the story for your newspaper.

_____

_____

_____

_____

_____

Faith Focus

How did the faith-filled women of the Old Testament help Mary?

With My Family

With your family's help, make a faith tree. On your faith tree, write the names of all the people who have helped your family to believe and trust in God.

Esther's Actions Show Her Faith

Living in a foreign land, Esther believed and trusted God. And so she asked God for the courage to help her people. Because of Esther's faith, the enemies of her people did not kill them. Years later Esther's people returned to their homeland. For them, Esther was a hero. She was a woman of faith.

Old Testament Women Teach Mary

Sarah and Hannah, Ruth and Esther believed and trusted God. Many years after they lived, an angel visited another faith-filled woman—Mary. The angel gave her a message from God. The angel announced that God wanted her to be the mother of Jesus, the Son of God. Mary said yes.

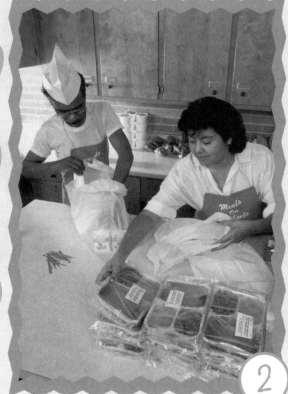

Hearing the stories of the faith-filled women of the Old Testament had helped Mary to become a woman of faith. Christians today continue to follow the examples of many of the faith-filled women of the Bible. These women show us how to believe and trust in God.

To Help You Remember

1. What does the story of Esther teach you about faith?

2. What do you think the story taught Mary?

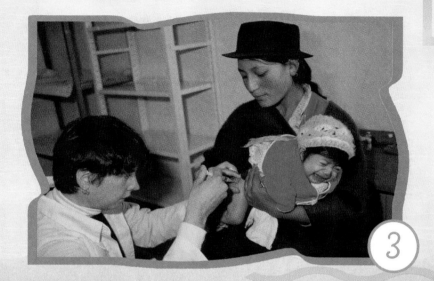

③

Living Our Faith

Look at the pictures on pages 44 and 45. They show people living their faith today in different ways. Choose one of the pictures and describe how the people are living their faith.

_____

_____

_____

_____

_____

Sarah, Hannah, Ruth, and Esther helped Mary to grow in her faith. The Church honors these faith-filled heroes of God. The Church also honors all the faith-filled followers of Jesus who have died. We call them saints.

Mother Teresa of Calcutta

Mother Teresa is known as the "Saint of the Gutters." For over 50 years she took care of the homeless, the sick, and the dying of Calcutta, India.

Mother Teresa started a new community of sisters called the Missionaries of Charity. She watched her community grow to over 4,000 sisters and 10,000 volunteers.

In 1979 Mother Teresa was given the Nobel Peace Prize because of her great love for and kindness to the poor and suffering. She followed the example of Mary's great faith by caring for others. In 1997 Mother Teresa died in Calcutta at the age of 87.

What can you learn from the example of the women of the Old Testament and Mother Teresa?

The stories of the women of faith of the Old Testament can help you trust in God's love for you too. Like Mary, you say yes to God because you trust God's love. You show your faith by the way you act and pray.

A Prayer to the Saints

Pray this prayer to the saints and to all holy women and men. Think about the stories of saints that you know and who are with God in heaven. Add their names to the prayer.

Blessed Sarah and Hannah, pray for us.

Blessed Esther and Ruth, pray for us.

Holy Mary, Mother of God, pray for us.

Saint _____, pray for us.

Saint _____, pray for us.

Saint _____, pray for us.

Saint _____, pray for us.

Amen.

My Faith Choice

This week I will speak my faith by praying. This week I will show my faith by

_____.

And now we pray.

God does wonderful things for those who trust in him. The LORD hears us when we pray.
Based on Psalm 4:4

Write *True* or *False* on the line before each statement.

_____F_____ 1. Sarah was the mother of Samuel.

_____F_____ 2. Hannah gave birth to a daughter.

_____T_____ 3. Ruth cared for Naomi.

_____F_____ 4. Esther lived in Egypt and saved her people there.

_____T_____ 5. Sarah, Hannah, Ruth, and Esther lived in faith.

Explain each of the following.

1. Explain what happened because Hannah believed in God's love. _Samuel was born_

2. Explain how Esther's faith saved her people. _The enemies did not_

3. Name one thing Mary, Jesus' mother, may have learned from Esther. _Have faith_

Think and share with your family.
Tell your family about Sarah, Hannah, Ruth, Esther, and Mary. Then list what you can do as a family to show your faith in God's love.

Visit our web site at www.FaithFirst.com

Jesus, the Son of God

5

We Pray

God of power
and mercy,
open our hearts in
welcome of receiving
Jesus with joy,
so that we may
become one with him
when he comes
in glory.
*Based on the Opening
Prayer for the Second
Sunday of Advent*

Jesus, God's Son
and our Savior, came
to share the good
news of God's love
with us. What stories
do you know about
Jesus?

*"In this way the love
of God was revealed
to us: God sent his only
Son into the world so
that we might have life
through him."*
1 John 4:9

Faith Vocabulary

Temple
The Temple is the holy place in Jerusalem where the Jewish people worshiped God.

Jerusalem
The holiest city of the Jewish people is Jerusalem.

Messiah
The word *messiah* means "anointed one." We believe that Jesus is the Anointed One promised by God.

When you were a baby, your family took you to church to be baptized. What a wonderful day that was! Through Baptism you now belong to Jesus and to the Christian community. Have you ever seen photographs of your baptism or heard stories about that special day?

Jesus, Our Messiah

When Jesus was a baby, Mary and Joseph took him to the **Temple** in the holy city of **Jerusalem.** When they arrived at the Temple, Mary and Joseph presented, or dedicated, Jesus to God.

At the Temple they met Simeon and Anna. Simeon had been waiting all his life for the **Messiah,** the One promised by God. Simeon took Jesus in his arms, blessed God, and said,

"O God, my eyes have now seen your salvation. Your salvation is a light for all people. Your salvation is glory for your people."

Based on Luke 2:30–32

Anna, too, had spent her life waiting for the Messiah. Like Simeon, she recognized Jesus as the One God had promised to send to save his people. The name *Jesus* means "God saves."

What a wonderful day that was for Mary and Joseph! We call this dedication of Jesus in the Temple the Presentation.

Who Is Jesus?

Simeon and Anna believed that Jesus was the Messiah promised by God. Follow the maze to lead Jesus, Mary, and Joseph to Simeon and Anna. Then write what you believe about Jesus.

To Help You Remember

1. Where did Mary and Joseph take Jesus to present him to God?

2. What did Simeon and Anna believe about Jesus?

With My Family

Simeon said that Jesus was a light for others. As a family, decide how you can be a light for others this week.

We do not know very much about the childhood of Jesus. We do know that Jesus grew up with Mary and Joseph in the small town of Nazareth. Here is the most famous story about Jesus' childhood.

The Boy Jesus in the Temple

When Jesus was twelve, the **Holy Family** went to Jerusalem to celebrate Passover as they did each year. Passover was a special Jewish feast that was celebrated in the Temple in Jerusalem.

When the great feast was over, Mary and Joseph began their journey home. Looking for Jesus, they realized that he was not with them. When they discovered Jesus was not traveling with their relatives, Mary and Joseph hurried back to Jerusalem to find him.

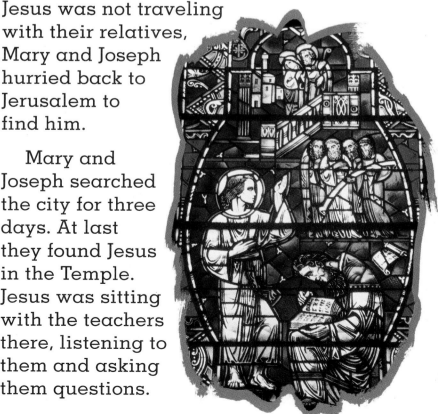

Mary and Joseph searched the city for three days. At last they found Jesus in the Temple. Jesus was sitting with the teachers there, listening to them and asking them questions.

Faith Focus

How did Jesus show obedience to Mary and Joseph?

Faith Vocabulary

Holy Family
Jesus, Mary, and Joseph are known as the Holy Family.

Jesus' understanding of the Sacred Scripture amazed the Temple teachers. After all, he was only a boy. "How did he become so wise?" the teachers wondered.

The Holy Family

Jesus returned home with Mary and Joseph. This is what the Gospel tells us.

> Obediently, Jesus went back home with Mary and Joseph. He remained obedient to them. As the years passed, Jesus grew in wisdom, age, and grace.
> Based on Luke 2:43–47 and 51–52

Mary, Joseph, and Jesus loved and respected one another. Jesus obeyed Mary and Joseph. Mary and Joseph shared their love for God with Jesus.

To Help You Remember

1. Why did the Holy Family go to Jerusalem?

2. Why did the boy Jesus seem so amazing to the Temple teachers?

Holy Families

Write or draw something you can do to help your family follow the example of the Holy Family.

Faith Vocabulary

kingdom of God
The time when people will live in peace and justice with God, one another, and all of God's creation is known as the kingdom of God.

disciples
The people who followed Jesus were called his disciples.

Gospel
The Good News Jesus came to proclaim is called the Gospel. The first four books of the New Testament are known as the Gospels.

Jesus Brings Good News

When Jesus grew up, he traveled from place to place. He preached about the **kingdom of God** and the good news that God loves all people.

Many people rejoiced at Jesus' good news. They became his **disciples** and followed him.

This is the story of how two of Jesus' disciples came to follow him.

One day Jesus was walking along the shore of the Sea of Galilee. He saw two brothers who were fishing. Their names were Simon and Andrew.

Jesus called out, "Follow me! I will teach you how to fish for people." The two brothers immediately followed Jesus.

Based on Mark 1:16–18

Jesus called others to follow him too. Jesus spent much of his time teaching his disciples to love and serve others as he loved and served them. Jesus' disciples believed the Good News, or the **Gospel,** of God's love. They came to believe that Jesus was the Son of God and the Messiah, the One who would save all people.

To Help You Remember

1. What is a disciple?

2. Why did the disciples come to believe that Jesus is the Messiah?

Being a Disciple

Through Baptism you are a disciple of Jesus. What have you learned about God's love? How do you serve others?

This Is What I Know About God's Love.

God gives us life

This Is How I Serve Others as a Disciple of Jesus.

We proclaim the Good News, or Gospel, by our actions as well as by our words. This was an idea that challenged the third grade class at Saint Monica's parish.

Good News in Action

The students wanted to put the Gospel into action. They thought about collecting food and clothing for the poor. They also considered having a neighborhood cleanup campaign and welcoming people who had just moved to the parish.

The third graders knew that all these actions would spread the Good News. Finally the class decided they could help the environment by cleaning up a nearby creek. They set a date and time. They went to local stores for donations, such as trash bags and work gloves. They made posters to get more people involved.

On the day of the cleanup, more than 50 people came to help. They filled 28 bags with trash. On the following day the students called the proper city department to have the bags collected.

The class agreed that their project was the Good News in action because gospel people are good stewards of all God's gifts.

How can you work with your friends to put the Gospel into action?

You are called by Jesus through Baptism to put the Gospel into action. You do this each time you read or listen to the gospel message. You do this each time you live as Jesus taught us to live.

Jesus' Message and Me

Complete the survey. Circle the things that you would be willing to do.

Ways I Can Listen and Respond to the Gospel Message

1. Help teach others the good news of God's love by trying to speak and act kindly.   **Yes**

2. Love others as Jesus loves by welcoming children who are new to my school or neighborhood.   **Yes**

3. Serve others as Jesus serves by offering to help out at home more often.   **Yes**

My Faith Choice

Choose one of your Yes responses that you will try to do this week. This week I will try to put the Gospel into action by

_____

_____ .

And now we pray.
"You are the Messiah, the Son of the living God."
Based on Matthew 16:16

CHAPTER REVIEW

Match the names and places in the left column
with their descriptions in the right column.

_a_ 1. Anna and Simeon

_d_ 2. disciples

_b_ 3. Jerusalem

_e_ 4. Temple

_c_ 5. Gospel

a. The people in the Temple who recognized Jesus as the long-awaited Messiah

b. The holy city of the Jewish people

c. The Good News of God's love

d. The people in the Gospel who were followers of Jesus

e. The holy place where the Jewish people worshiped God

Complete the sentences.

1. The Anointed One promised by God is called the _messiah_ .

2. The ceremony in which the baby Jesus was dedicated to God is known as the _presentation_ .

3. The time when people will live in peace and justice with God, one another, and all of God's creation is known as the _kingdom of god_ .

4. The _Holy Family_ is the family of Mary, Joseph, and Jesus.

Think and share with your family.

Take time this week to discuss the Sunday gospel reading as a family. Be sure to include ideas of how the message of the Gospel can be lived out in your home or community.

The Death and Resurrection of Jesus

6

We Pray

God our Father,
by raising Christ
your Son
you conquered
the power of death
and opened
for us the way
to eternal life.
*Opening Prayer
for Easter Sunday*

Jesus died on a cross, was raised to new life, and returned to his Father in heaven. What do you know about these wonderful events?

Christ has died, Christ is risen, Christ will come again.

What kinds of feelings do you have when someone hurts you? How do you act? Do you find it easy to forgive the one who hurt you?

Jesus Dies on a Cross

One night a crowd of people arrested Jesus. They brought him to Pilate, the Roman governor. He ordered Jesus to be beaten and **crucified,** or put to death on a cross.

This is what happened that day.

SOLDIERS:	*(leading Jesus out of Jerusalem)* Hurry along there!
WOMEN:	*(standing along the road)* We are so sorry this is happening to you, Jesus!
JESUS' ENEMIES:	*(laughing at him as the soldiers nail him to the cross)* Ha! Ha! You saved others! Save yourself now! Ha! Ha!
JESUS:	Father, forgive them for they do not know what they are doing. *(Time passes. It is now three o'clock in the afternoon.)*
JESUS:	Father, I give myself to you.

After Jesus died, one of his followers buried his body in a tomb.

Based on Luke 23:26–27, 33–35, 42–43, 46, 50, and 53

Faith Focus

What did Jesus say on the cross that showed his love for all people?

Faith Vocabulary

crucified
To be crucified means to be put to death on a cross.

Good Friday
Good Friday is the Friday before Easter Sunday. It is the day when we remember that Jesus was crucified and died.

Jesus is our Savior. He suffered and died on the cross to save all people from their sins. His death on the cross was a sacrifice for our sins. Jesus loved us so much that he gave his life for us so we could live with him in heaven. We call the day Jesus died on the cross **Good Friday.**

Jesus chose to love and forgive those who hurt him and put him to death. Jesus showed us, his followers, how we are to love and forgive one another.

To Help You Remember

1. What do we remember on Good Friday?

2. How did Jesus treat those who hurt him and put him to death?

With My Family

As a family, make a cross to remember Jesus' love for you and for all people. Print Jesus' words of forgiveness on the cross. Put your family's cross in a special place.

Choose to Follow Jesus

Check [✔] those statements that you will choose because you are a follower of Jesus. Then write a statement of your own.

_____ 1. When someone hurts me, I can choose to forgive.

___✓___ 2. When I need help, I will trust Jesus to be with me.

___✓___ 3. When someone needs my help, I can lend a helping hand.

___✓___ 4. When I am lonely or scared, I can remember that God loves me.

___✓___ 5. When I am filled with joy, I can share my joy with others.

6. When _____

_____

Faith Vocabulary

Resurrection
God's raising Jesus from the dead to new life by the power of the Holy Spirit is called the Resurrection.

Easter
Easter is the time of the year Christians celebrate and remember the Resurrection of Jesus.

Paschal mystery
The suffering, death, and Resurrection of Jesus is known as his Paschal mystery.

When someone we love dies, we feel very sad. We might cry. We might want to be with others, or we might want to be alone. Losing the person we loved is all we can think about. Sadness and pain are all we can feel.

God Raises Jesus to New Life

Jesus' friends lost someone they loved when Jesus died on the cross. Here is their story.

Three days after Jesus died, some of the women disciples went to his tomb. Suddenly, a great earthquake shook the ground. An angel rolled back the stone that covered Jesus' tomb. The women were afraid.

ANGEL: Do not be afraid. Jesus is not here.

WOMEN: Where is he?

ANGEL: God has raised him from the dead! Go quickly and tell the other disciples!

(The women run to tell the other disciples. On their way they meet the Risen Jesus. Their sadness changes to joy!)

WOMEN: Jesus? Is it you?

JESUS: Do not be afraid! Tell the others that they will see me in Galilee.

Based on Matthew 28:1–10

We celebrate the **Resurrection** of Jesus on **Easter.** Easter is our greatest feast because Jesus won for us the promise of life with God forever. We believe that we too shall live after we die. We will live in happiness with God forever.

Jesus' suffering, death, and Resurrection are known as the **Paschal mystery.** We are called to share the joy of Jesus' Resurrection with all people.

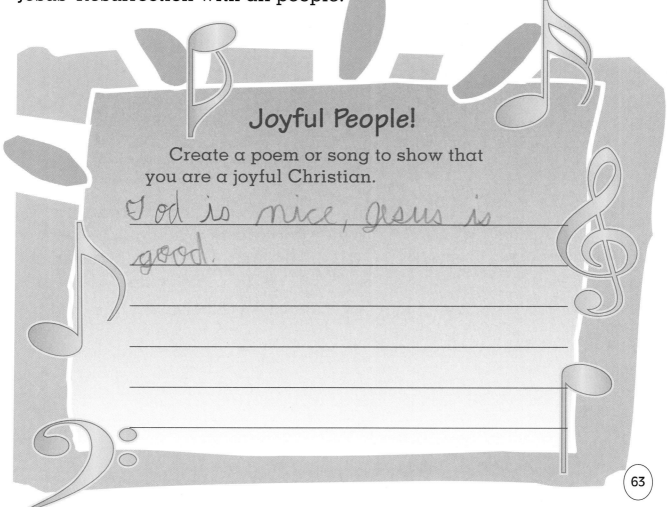

Joyful People!

Create a poem or song to show that you are a joyful Christian.

God is nice, Jesus is good.

Faith Focus

What did the Risen Jesus do after spending time with his friends?

Faith Vocabulary

Ascension

The return of the Risen Jesus to his Father is called the Ascension.

Has anyone you loved ever gone away for a while and then returned? Do you remember how happy you were to see that person again? You probably wanted to spend a lot of time with him or her. You might even have said, "Please don't ever go away again!"

Jesus Returns to His Father

Jesus' disciples felt much the same way after Jesus' death and Resurrection. They wanted Jesus to be with them always.

The Risen Jesus stayed with his disciples for 40 days after the Resurrection. He promised them that God would soon send the Holy Spirit to them. The Holy Spirit would help them to remember all that Jesus had taught them.

Then one day Jesus led his disciples out to the town of Bethany. He blessed them and was taken up into heaven.

Based on Luke 24:50–51

We call Jesus' return to his Father the **Ascension.** One day we too will return to our Father in heaven.

With You Always

The disciples returned to Jerusalem and praised God each day in the Temple. The Holy Spirit came to them, and they were given the power to speak bravely about God's kingdom to all those they met.

To Help You Remember

1. What would the disciples be able to do with the help of the Holy Spirit?

2. Why do you think the apostles rejoiced when Jesus ascended to his Father?

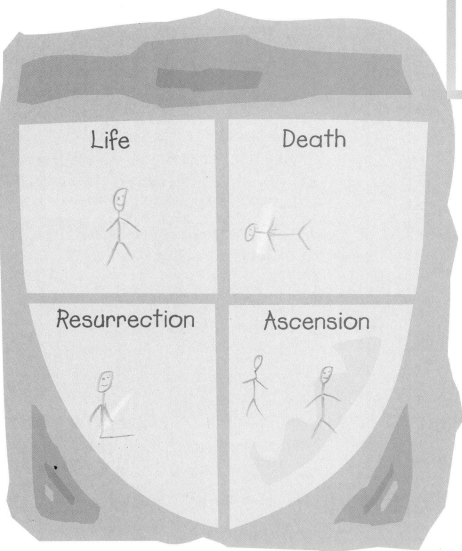

Life

Death

Resurrection

Ascension

Remembering Jesus' Love for Us

Design this emblem with pictures or words that tell about Jesus' life, death, Resurrection, and Ascension. Then write one way you can live as a joyful follower of Christ.

_____

_____

_____

_____

When we celebrate the Paschal mystery, we remember the suffering, death, and Resurrection of Jesus.

The Way of the Cross

The Way of the Cross, or Stations of the Cross, helps us to remember Jesus' death and Resurrection. Many churches have the fourteen Stations of the Cross on their church walls. The Stations of the Cross are prayed by Catholics especially during the season of Lent.

First Station

Fifth Station

Twelfth Station

1. Jesus is condemned to death.
2. Jesus accepts his cross.
3. Jesus falls the first time.
4. Jesus meets his mother.
5. Simon helps Jesus to carry the cross.
6. Veronica wipes the face of Jesus.
7. Jesus falls the second time.
8. Jesus meets the women.
9. Jesus falls the third time.
10. Jesus is stripped of his clothes.
11. Jesus is nailed to the cross.
12. Jesus dies on the cross.
13. Jesus is taken down from the cross.
14. Jesus is buried in the tomb.

Many churches now include a fifteenth station.

15. Jesus is raised from the dead.

What do the Stations of the Cross look like in your church?

You can remember the Paschal mystery of Jesus too. You can show that you remember Jesus' death, Resurrection, and Ascension by the way you live.

Plan Ahead

I, _Victor Bonilla_ ,

pledge to remember what Jesus did for me by living as a true Christian.

When I see someone who is sad, I will _cheer them up_ .

When I see someone who is hurting, I will _I will be there for them_ .

When I see someone who is angry, I will _calm them down_ .

When I see someone who is lonely, I will _join them_ .

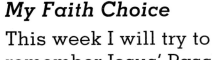

My Faith Choice

This week I will try to remember Jesus' Paschal mystery by doing what I have written on my Plan Ahead chart.

And now we pray.

Lord Jesus, you are the Savior of the world.
Based on the Memorial Acclamation

Circle the correct words to complete each sentence.

1. God raised Jesus from the dead on
    Ascension Thursday.
    Pentecost.
    (Easter.)

2. Jesus' returning to his Father is called the
    death and dying of Jesus.
    Resurrection.
    (Ascension.)

3. Jesus' being raised to new life is known as the
    Crucifixion.
    Ascension.
    (Resurrection.)

4. Jesus' suffering, dying, and being raised to new life
    are known as the
    (Paschal mystery.)
    Ascension.
    coming of the Holy Spirit.

Unscramble the letters to complete the sentences.

1. Jesus promised his Father would send the (olhy) H O L Y

   (pirsti) S p i r i t when Jesus returned to heaven.

2. This happened 40 days after the Resurrection.

   (scasnioen) A s c e n s i o n

3. Another name for the day Jesus was raised from the dead is

   the (srcreterioun) R e s u r r e c t i o n.

Think and share with your family.

Visit your parish church with your family. Talk about each Station of the Cross. Then pray the Stations of the Cross as a family.

Visit our
web site at
www.FaithFirst.com

The Holy Spirit

A Scripture Story

7

We Pray

Come, Holy Spirit,
fill the hearts
of your faithful.
And kindle in them
the fire of your love.
*Traditional Prayer
to the Holy Spirit*

The Holy Spirit is
with us at every
moment of every day.
What do you know
about the Holy Spirit?

*Stained-glass window
of the dove, a symbol for
the Holy Spirit.*

Bible Background

Faith Focus

What promise did Jesus make to his disciples at the Last Supper?

Faith Vocabulary

Last Supper
The Last Supper is the special meal that Jesus and his disciples ate together on the night before he died.

Wind and fire are also symbols for the Holy Spirit.

Sometimes people promise us good things. We look forward to receiving what was promised. What was the best promise anyone ever made to you?

Jesus Promises the Spirit

Jesus made a special promise to his disciples. They looked forward to receiving what Jesus promised. This is how it happened.

Before he died, Jesus shared a special meal with his followers. We call this meal the **Last Supper.** During the meal Jesus told his friends that he was going to return to his Father. Then he told them not to worry or be sad. He made a promise to them.

Jesus promised that God would send the Holy Spirit to his followers. The Holy Spirit would help them to remember all that Jesus taught them. The Spirit would always be with them. They would never be alone.

After Jesus died, was raised from the dead, and returned to his Father in heaven, the disciples returned to Jerusalem. There they waited for the coming of the Holy Spirit.

Dear Friend,

I'm one of Jesus' disciples and I feel very happy because he promise to be with us forever and ever

The Promise of Jesus

Imagine that you are one of Jesus' disciples waiting in Jerusalem for the Holy Spirit to come as Jesus promised. Write a letter to a friend. Tell your friend about Jesus' promise. Describe how you feel and what you are hoping for.

Faith Vocabulary

Holy Spirit
The third Person of the Holy Trinity is the Holy Spirit.

Pentecost
Pentecost is the day on which the Holy Spirit came upon the disciples in Jerusalem.

We trust people who keep their promises. The disciples knew they could trust Jesus. He loved them, and he would keep his promise. So they waited, knowing his promise would come true.

The Spirit Comes on Pentecost

The **Holy Spirit** came to the disciples on the Jewish feast of **Pentecost.** This happened 50 days after God raised Jesus to new life. The New Testament tells us about the coming of the Holy Spirit.

The disciples were gathered in a house when suddenly, a sound like a strong wind filled the room. Small flames of fire seemed to settle over each disciple's head. The disciples went out into the streets. They saw many people who had come to Jerusalem for Pentecost.

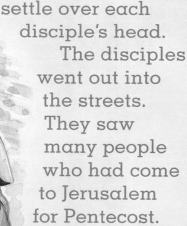

Jesus' disciples, especially their leader Peter, began to speak to the people. The disciples wanted everyone to know that God had raised Jesus to new life!

All the people spoke in different languages. Yet everyone understood what the disciples were saying. The Holy Spirit helped them to understand. Many people came to believe in Jesus on that day.

Based on Acts of the Apostles 2:1–41

The Holy Spirit helped the disciples to teach the people about Jesus. The Spirit helped them to spread the good news of Jesus' Resurrection.

The Spirit Alive!

In each flame of fire, write a quality or characteristic that would help you to tell other people about Jesus.

Faith Focus

How does the Holy Spirit help us?

Faith Vocabulary

Advocate

Advocate is a name for the Holy Spirit that means "one who speaks for someone else."

With My Family

Use the names for the Holy Spirit to write a family prayer. Pray your prayer together every day.

The Holy Spirit Is with Us

Jesus told his followers that they would never be alone. The Holy Spirit would always be with them. We trust Jesus. We believe that the Holy Spirit is with us today and tomorrow and always.

The Holy Spirit helped Jesus' disciples. We believe that the Spirit helps us too. And so we give the Holy Spirit many names that show our belief that the Holy Spirit is always with us. These names help us to understand God's great gift to us.

Our Names for the Holy Spirit

Advocate. An advocate is a person who speaks for us. An advocate defends us. The Holy Spirit speaks for us to God. The Spirit defends us against danger and evil.

Helper. A helper is a person who helps us when we need aid. The Holy Spirit comes to our aid when life is hard.

Guide. A guide is a person who shows us the way. The Holy Spirit shows us the way to follow Jesus.

The Holy Spirit is the third Person of the Holy Trinity. The Spirit helps us to know and love God. The Spirit is our advocate, our helper, and our guide.

To Help You Remember

1. What are three names for the Holy Spirit?

2. How does the Spirit help us?

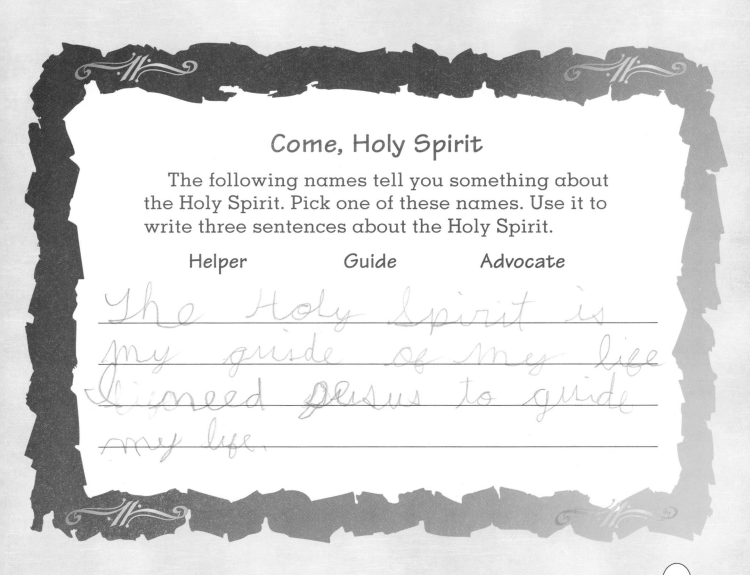

Come, Holy Spirit

The following names tell you something about the Holy Spirit. Pick one of these names. Use it to write three sentences about the Holy Spirit.

Helper   Guide   Advocate

The Holy Spirit is my guide of my life. I need Jesus to guide my life.

Jesus promised that the Holy Spirit would always be with us. Since Pentecost the Spirit has guided the Church.

Signs of the Holy Spirit

We use symbols to help us understand the Holy Spirit. Often we see these symbols in our churches. Fire and wind are two symbols for the Holy Spirit that help us remember the Pentecost story.

The Holy Spirit helps us to grow as members of the Christian family. The New Testament names nine "signs" that show the Spirit is at work in our lives. These signs are called the fruits of the Holy Spirit.

Look at the fruits of the Holy Spirit listed in the banner. Talk about one way you can practice each one.

LOVE

PEACE

KINDNESS

JOY

GENEROSITY

FAITHFULNESS

PATIENCE

GENTLENESS

SELF-CONTROL

from Galatians 5:22

The Holy Spirit is with you today. The Spirit will be with you tomorrow, next week, and next month. The Spirit will be with you next year and when you are all grown up. You can count on the Spirit. The Holy Spirit will always be your friend.

Talking to God

Imagine that you need to do something, but you do not know how to begin. Write the prayer you would say to the Spirit to ask for help. Use simple words to tell the Spirit what you need.

_____

_____

_____

_____

Keep this prayer where you can see it.

My Faith Choice

This week I will remember that the Spirit is with me. I will ask the Holy Spirit to help me when I

_____ .

And now we pray.

Father of light, send your Spirit into our lives.
Based on Alternative Opening Prayer for Pentecost

Using the words in the box, complete the following sentences.

| Last Supper | Holy Spirit | Pentecost |
| Peter | Advocate | |

1. Jesus made a promise to his disciples at the
   Last Supper.

2. The Holy Spirit came to the disciples on the feast
   of _Pentecost_.

3. _Peter_ and the other disciples talked
   to the people on Pentecost.

4. The name _Advocate_ means "one who
   speaks for someone else."

5. Helper and Guide are two names we use for the
   Holy Spirit.

Answer the following questions.

1. How did Jesus keep his promise to his disciples?
   by giving the
   Last Supper

2. How did the Holy Spirit help Peter and the other disciples?
   _____
   _____

Think and share with your family.
Get a small notebook and begin
to keep a journal about how the
Holy Spirit helps your family.

Visit our
web site at
www.FaithFirst.com

We Are
the Church

We Pray

God our Father,
may your Church
always be
your holy people.
*Mass for
Universal Church*

The Church is the
People of God. You
are a member of the
Church. How do you
act as a member of
the Church?

*Christians gather
to worship God each
Sunday.*

We Are Followers of Christ

Faith Focus

How did the early Christians follow Jesus' example?

Faith Vocabulary

Church
The Church is the People of God.

When have you been chosen to do a special job or to deliver a special message? When that happens, it is important to be responsible and get the job done as well as you can.

Jesus Gives a Command

After Jesus' Resurrection from the dead, he gave an important responsibility to his followers. This is what he said to them.

"Go to the people of all nations and make them my disciples. Baptize them in the name of the Father, and of the Son, and of the Holy Spirit. Teach them everything I have told you. I will be with you always."

Based on Matthew 28:18–20

Jesus' disciples did just that. Many people were baptized and became followers of Jesus. Every day the community of believers grew.

In the Acts of the Apostles we read about the first Christian communities. These communities made up the early **Church.**

Jesus' followers spent their time learning from the apostles. They lived like a family. They broke bread and prayed together.

The community of believers shared all things in common. They sold their property and possessions. Then they gave the money to whoever needed it. Because they shared, everyone had all they needed.

Every day the Lord added to their group others who believed.

Based on Acts of the Apostles 2:42–47

The Catholic Church goes all the way back to the apostles. Today we continue to try to follow Jesus as the early Christians did. In our parish communities we gather to pray. We share with those who are in need. We help others to know about Jesus and the Good News of God's love for all people.

To Help You Remember

1. What did Jesus ask his disciples to do?

2. How did the early Christians live?

With My Family

List some ways you live today as a family who follows Jesus. Discuss how your family can share the Good News with other families.

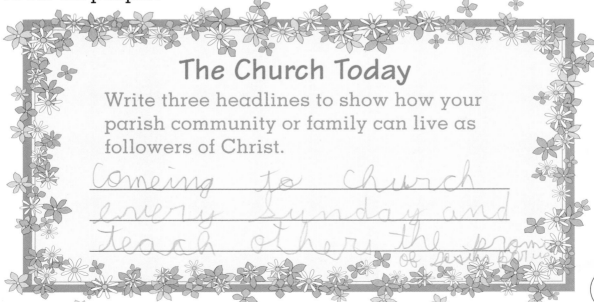

The Church Today

Write three headlines to show how your parish community or family can live as followers of Christ.

Comeing to church every Sunday and teach others the

Baptism Makes Us Christians

The Church continues to follow Jesus' command to baptize people of every nation. The Church welcomes its new members in the **Sacraments of Initiation.** The word *initiation* means "to make a person a member of a group." The Sacraments of Initiation are **Baptism,** Confirmation, and Eucharist.

Sarah's Baptism

I was only a baby when my family brought me to the Church to be baptized. They said that they believed in God the Father and in Jesus Christ and in the Holy Spirit. They promised to share their faith with me and to help me live as Jesus taught.

Faith Focus

How do we become members of the Church?

Faith Vocabulary

Sacraments of Initiation
The Sacraments of Initiation join us to Christ and welcome us into the church community. There are three Sacraments of Initiation. They are Baptism, Confirmation, and Eucharist.

Baptism
Baptism is the sacrament in which we are joined to Christ. Through Baptism we become members of the Church and followers of Jesus, our sins are forgiven, and we receive the gift of the Holy Spirit.

The priest first made the sign of the cross on my head and claimed me for Jesus. I would now belong to Jesus forever! The priest, while pouring water on my head, said, "Sarah, I baptize you in the name of the Father, and of the Son, and of the Holy Spirit."

The water was a sign that I now had new life in Christ. I was marked as a follower of Christ forever. Our baptism lasts forever. That is why we can be baptized only one time.

Next the priest anointed my head with holy oil called chrism. This was a sign of my special calling to live as a follower of Jesus. Then he put a white garment on me to show that I had put on the new life of Christ. Finally the priest lighted a candle from the large Easter candle and gave it to my parents and godparents. The lighted candle was given as a reminder that I was to follow Jesus, the Light of the World.

To Help You Remember

1. What do we call the sacraments that welcome us into the Church?

2. How do we become members of the Church and followers of Jesus?

Signs of Baptism

Water, a white garment, and a lighted candle are all signs of Baptism. Tell in your own words what each sign of Baptism means.

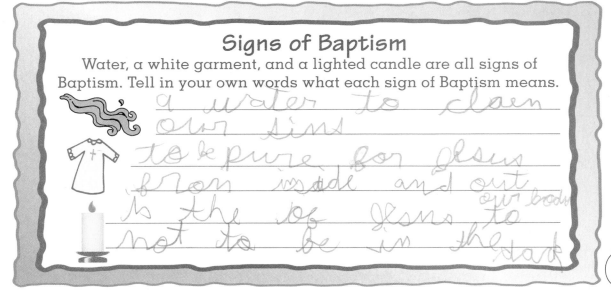

a water to clean our sins

to be pure for Jesus from inside and out our body

is the be Jesus to not to be in the dark

Faith Focus

How does the sacrament of Confirmation help us to follow Jesus?

Faith Vocabulary

Confirmation

Confirmation is the Sacrament of Initiation in which baptized people receive and celebrate the strengthening of the gift of the Spirit within them.

Confirmation Strengthens the Spirit's Gifts Within Us

Confirmation is another Sacrament of Initiation. By celebrating Confirmation with the church community, we are strengthened to live as Jesus' followers through the gift of the Holy Spirit.

The usual minister of the sacrament of Confirmation is a bishop. Bishop Perry would like to tell you about Confirmation.

Celebrating Confirmation

It is always a privilege for me to visit the parishes of my diocese and celebrate the sacrament of Confirmation with the young people there. And sometimes the people are not so young!

The sacrament of Confirmation usually takes place within the Mass. After the Gospel I give a short homily about the meaning of Confirmation. Then I ask the candidates to renew their baptismal promises. After that I stand in front of the candidates for Confirmation and extend my hands over them. I pray, "Send your Spirit upon them to be their Helper and Guide."

Then, one by one, the candidates join me near the altar with their sponsors. I dip my thumb into a dish of holy oil called chrism. I rest my right hand on each candidate's head while I make the sign of the cross on his or her forehead with the chrism and pray, "Be sealed with the Gift of the Holy Spirit." The candidate answers, "Amen."

The candidates are now confirmed Catholics and are called to bring Jesus to the world. The Holy Spirit will be with them to help them make good choices and live as followers of Christ.

Like Baptism, we can receive Confirmation only one time. We receive the seal of the Holy Spirit that marks us as followers of Jesus.

To Help You Remember

1. Who is the usual minister of the sacrament of Confirmation?

2. Explain what the bishop does at Confirmation.

Growing Strong

Imagine that it is the day of your Confirmation. Name three ways you will "bring Jesus to the world" as a confirmed Catholic.

1. _____

2. _____

3. _____

Through Baptism we are joined with Jesus Christ and become members of the Church. As followers of Jesus Christ we are called to love God and one another. We show this by our words and our actions.

The Church Today

The Church today is made up of so many people helping and caring for one another. Being active members of our Church assists us in being faithful followers of Jesus Christ. The way we act, the things we say, and even our attitudes show our love for God and others.

The Church today also helps us to be strong, hopeful, and peaceful people. Living as a follower of Jesus Christ allows us to know and share God's love.

Talk about how the picture and headlines show Christians living as followers of Jesus today.

SAINT ANTHONY'S Soup Kitchen

Serving: Tuesday, Thursday & Friday

Hours: 4:30 To 5:30 PM

Parish Teens Collect for Clothing Drive

Parish Volunteers Paint Homeless Shelter

Third Graders Bring Plants to Nursing Home

Students Sponsor Car Wash for Missionary Fund

What Difference Does It Make in My Life?

You have already celebrated at least one of the Sacraments of Initiation. You are a member of the Church. Each day you try your best to live as a follower of Jesus.

Receiving the Sacraments of Initiation

Design a card for someone who will be receiving one of the Sacraments of Initiation. Tell the person why you think this is such a wonderful thing.

My Faith Choice

This week when I have a decision to make, I will try to think about what a baptized Christian would do.

And now we pray.

Father,
send your Holy Spirit
upon us
to be our helper
and guide.

Based on Rite of Confirmation

Match the words in column A with their meanings in column B.

Column A

___a___ 1. Christian

___c___ 2. Church

___b___ 3. Confirmation

___d___ 4. Baptism

Column B

a. A person who is baptized and believes in and follows Jesus Christ

b. The People of God

c. The sacrament in which we are joined to Christ, become members of the Church, our sins are forgiven, and we receive the gift of the Holy Spirit

d. The sacrament in which baptized people receive and celebrate the strengthening of the the gift of the Holy Spirit within them

Write a paragraph to explain either the sacrament of Baptism or the sacrament of Confirmation.

The sacrament of Baptism is to accept Jesus in our body.

Think and share with your family.

Talk with your family about the day you were baptized. Ask your family any questions you might have about that day.

Visit our web site at www.FaithFirst.com

The Communion of Saints

9

We Pray

God our Father,
the work of your
hands and the
beauty of your truth
shine brightly
in your saints.
May we be filled
with the same Spirit
that blessed
their lives so that we
also may know
their peace.

*Based on the
Opening Prayer for the
Feast of All Saints*

Our world has
many heroes. Who
are some of the
Church's heroes?

*The communion
of saints includes the
faithful on earth. You
are a member of the
communion of saints.*

Faith Focus

What is the communion of saints?

Faith Vocabulary

saints

The saints are people whose love for God is stronger than anything else. The Church honors some people who have died by naming them saints.

communion of saints

The community of the followers of Jesus, both those living on earth and in heaven, is known as the communion of saints.

When you hear the word *saint*, what do you think of? Maybe you think of someone who prays all day. Or maybe you think of a person you know who seems to have a special friendship with God.

Saints Are God's Heroes

Saints are people whose love for God is stronger than anything else. Through prayer and kind acts, they show their love for God and for other people. Mary, the mother of Jesus, is our most holy saint.

The Communion of Saints

In the Apostles' Creed we pray, "I believe in the Holy Spirit, the holy catholic Church, the **communion of saints,** the forgiveness of sins, the resurrection of the body, and the life everlasting. Amen."

The communion of saints is made up of people who are living and people who have died. It includes people living on earth who are trying to live holy lives. It also includes people who are living with God in heaven.

Some people who die are not ready to receive the gift of heaven. These people also belong to the communion of saints. For they too are growing in their love for God and will live with God forever in heaven.

All these people form a communion, or the community of God's holy people. We believe that we can pray to the saints who live with God in heaven. We can also pray for people who have died who are getting ready to live with God in heaven forever.

Interview with a Saint

Pretend you are a reporter planning to interview a saint. Write the name of the saint and three or four questions you would ask him or her.

Faith Vocabulary

feasts
Special days of the church year that are put aside to honor the saints are called feasts.

patron saints
Saints who have been chosen to pray in a special way for people, countries, parishes, and for other reasons are called patron saints.

The Church Honors Saints

Our country honors heroes. The Church too honors its heroes, the saints. We honor them for their holiness. We believe that they show us through their lives how we can live lives that are holy. They also show us that we too will live with God and all the saints when we die if we live holy lives. Whenever we live and love as Jesus taught us, we are living holy lives.

One way the Church honors saints for their holiness is to set aside special days called **feasts.** On these days the Church honors the saints by recalling their lives on earth and remembering how they followed Jesus.

The Mass that is celebrated on the feast of a saint includes prayers that ask the saint to pray for us and with us. By honoring the saints in this way, the Church helps us to remember what it means to live as children of God.

Some Places Named for Saints

SAINT HELENS

SAINT AGATHA

SAINT PAUL

SAINT LOUIS

SAINT MARYS

SAINT MICHAEL

SAN FRANCISCO

SAINT ANDREWS

SAINT GEORGE

SAINT AUGUSTINE

SAN ANTONIO

SAINT BERNARD

Patron Saints

The Church also names certain holy people as **patron saints.** You may have a patron saint for whom you were named at Baptism, or your parish may be named for a particular saint. Patron saints are called on to pray in a special way for countries, towns and cities, and local churches. Specific groups of people, such as carpenters and teachers, also have patron saints.

The map of the United States on page 92 shows some of the places in our country that have been named for saints. Are there other places in your state that have saints' names?

The map of the United States on page 92

Your Parish Church

What is the name of your parish church?

The name of My p

Who is your church named after?

_____

Is there a special statue, picture, or window that honors who your church is named for? What does it tell you?

_____
_____
_____
_____
_____

Faith Vocabulary

Body of Christ
Another name for the Church is the Body of Christ.

With My Family

Make a family saints' book. Find out information about the lives of saints for whom you and your family members were named. Write or draw what you discover about each saint in your family book of saints.

Do you remember how the early Christians lived in a community? They shared all their possessions and talents with one another. They shared the Body and Blood of Christ. As members of the Church, they cared for one another.

The Eucharist Makes Us One

At Mass we share in the Eucharist, the Body and Blood of Christ. When we receive the Body and Blood of Christ in the Eucharist, we are joined most fully to Jesus and to one another. We are the **Body of Christ** in the world.

As the Body of Christ, we unite our actions with those of Jesus. We continue today the work Jesus began long ago, such as feeding the hungry and comforting the lonely. The Holy Spirit helps the entire communion of saints, or Body of Christ, work together. We work together to bring God's love and life to everyone.

To help people understand how we are the Body of Christ, Saint Paul wrote a letter to the people of Corinth who were trying to live as a community of Jesus' followers. This is part of what Paul told them.

> The body of Christ has many parts, just as any human body does. But we were all baptized in the same Spirit. This made us all members of Christ's body. Together we are the body of Christ. Each of us is an important part of his body.
>
> Based on 1 Corinthians 12:12–13, 27

Each member of the Body of Christ has different gifts and talents. Each of us is an important part of Christ's Body, the Church.

To Help You Remember

1. What does Paul mean by the Body of Christ?

2. How does the Eucharist help unite the communion of saints?

Many Gifts, One Body

What gifts do you have to share with the other members of the Church, the Body of Christ? Complete the sentences below by telling how you could help build up the Body of Christ.

With my eyes, I can _____.

With my mouth, I can _____.

With my hands, I can _____.

With my feet, I can _____.

With my ears, I can _____.

The Church is the communion of saints. It is the community of the followers of Christ. It is the Body of Christ in the world.

Our Lady of Guadalupe

The Church celebrates feast days in honor of the saints. Mary, the mother of Jesus, is the greatest saint of the Church. One of the great feasts in the church year that honors Mary is the feast of Our Lady of Guadalupe. This is a very special feast day for the people of Mexico, where the city of Guadalupe is located.

The Church celebrates this feast to remember the story of Juan Diego and how he spoke with a beautiful Aztec woman who told him she was Mary, the Mother of God. Mary's appearance to Juan Diego helps us believe that God's love is for everyone. People of every race and language are loved by God.

On the feast of Our Lady of Guadalupe, December 12, we honor Mary as the patron saint of the Americas. Many parishes have celebrations that include music and fine foods.

If you could ask Mary, the Mother of God, one question, what would it be?

You, along with Mary and the other saints, belong to the communion of saints. Following the example of the saints can help you live as a follower of Jesus.

Patron Saints

Read about the saints who are patrons of children and students. You can pray to these saints to help and guide you.

Saint Nicholas is the patron saint of children. He always had a special love for children because he was an orphan. When he grew up, Nicholas went about showing children how much God loves them.

Saint Thomas Aquinas always enjoyed learning. He studied very hard. When Thomas grew up, he became a Dominican friar. Thomas spent his life praying, studying, and teaching others about Jesus. Thomas Aquinas is the patron saint of students.

Find out about another patron saint. Share what you have learned with your class.

My Faith Choice

This week I will ask my favorite saint to help me. I will pray to Saint _____ for help.

I will ask this saint to help me _____ .

And now we pray.

Father, hear our prayers. Unite all your children wherever they may be.

Based on Eucharistic Prayer III

Use the clues to complete this crossword puzzle.

DOWN

1. The call to serve God in a special way
2. A saint who has been chosen to pray in a special way for people, countries, and parishes
4. Days in the church year that are set aside to honor the saints
5. People honored by the Church for their holiness

ACROSS

3. The followers of Jesus, both on earth and in heaven

Answer the following questions.

1. Who belongs to the communion of saints?

_____

2. How does the Church honor saints?

_____

3. What does it mean to be a member of the Body of Christ? _____

Think and share with your family.

How does the Catholic tradition of remembering and honoring the saints help our family to remember and honor Jesus?

Visit our web site at www.FaithFirst.com

Paul: Jesus' Special Apostle

A Scripture Story

Paul was called to be an apostle. What do you know about Saint Paul?

Stained-glass window showing Saint Paul the Apostle.

Bible Background

Faith Focus

Why did Saul want to arrest the followers of Jesus?

Faith Vocabulary

Pharisee

A Pharisee was one of a group of Jewish leaders who followed the Law of Moses as closely as possible.

Law of Moses

The Law of Moses was the Ten Commandments plus other important laws that guided the Jewish people.

Stephen

Stephen was the first Christian who died for his faith.

Sometimes when we love something very much, we become sad if someone wants to change it or take it away. Long ago a Jewish man named Saul, who loved his Jewish faith very much, thought that the followers of Jesus were changing his religion.

Who Was Saint Paul?

Saul was a **Pharisee** who followed all the laws and customs of his people. The **Law of Moses** guided his life. He himself became an important teacher. People listened to him and did what he said.

Saul came to Jerusalem after the Risen Jesus returned to his Father. While he lived there, Saul heard all about Jesus and what Jesus' disciples were teaching. This upset Saul because he thought Jesus' disciples were speaking against the Law of Moses.

Saul questions Christians.

One day Saul watched while **Stephen,** one of Jesus' followers, was stoned to death because he was a Christian. Saul disliked what Jesus' followers were teaching. He thought that they did not follow the Law of Moses, which he loved so much. So Saul went about looking for followers of Jesus. He wanted to arrest them and bring them back to Jerusalem and put them on trial.

To Help You Remember

1. What did Saul become when he grew up?

2. Why did he dislike what the Christians were teaching?

Questioning a Christian

Imagine that you are Saul and that you have arrested a Christian in Jerusalem. Write down one question you will ask this Christian. Then write down what you think this Christian will answer.

Saul's question:

_____

_____

_____

_____

_____

The Christian's answer:

_____

_____

_____

_____

_____

Reading the Word of God

Faith Focus

What happened to change Saul so that he became a follower of Jesus?

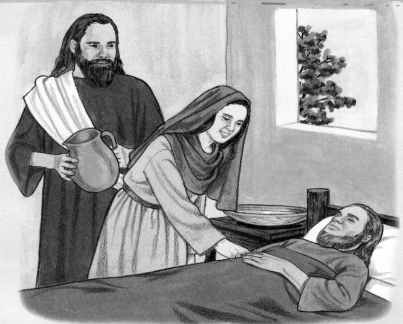

Ananias with Saul in Damascus.

Faith Vocabulary

Ananias
Ananias was a follower of Jesus who lived in Damascus; through God's power he healed Saul's blindness.

Paul
Paul was the name that Saul took after he became a follower of Jesus.

conversion
The experience of changing one's heart and turning back to God is called conversion.

Have you ever changed your mind about anything? Long ago Saul did. God helped him to change everything in his life!

Jesus Calls Saul

One day Saul left Jerusalem and traveled toward Damascus. Suddenly, a great light shone around him. Saul fell to the ground and heard a voice speaking to him.

VOICE: Saul, why are you hurting me?

SAUL: Who are you?

VOICE: I am Jesus. When you hurt my followers, you hurt me. Get up and go into Damascus. Someone will help you there.

NARRATOR: Saul gets up, but he is blind. His companions lead him into the city. Three days later Ananias, a follower of Jesus, comes to Saul. Ananias lays his hands on Saul.

ANANIAS: Saul, God gives you the gift of the Holy Spirit.

NARRATOR: Suddenly, Saul sees again.

SAUL: Praise be to God!

NARRATOR: Saul believes in the Risen Jesus. So Ananias baptizes him. Saul then begins to preach the good news of God's love.

Based on Acts of the Apostles 9:1–20

Saul then became known as **Paul.** He changed from being a nonbeliever to being a believer. We call this his **conversion.** Each year the Church celebrates Saul's conversion on January 25.

To Help You Remember

1. Why did Saul go to Damascus?

2. How do you think Saul felt when he heard Jesus speak to him?

With My Family

Act out the story of Saul with your family. Use props and sing a song to praise God for Saul's conversion.

Paul Meets a Christian in Jerusalem

Imagine that you are Paul. You are back again in Jerusalem. Now you, too, are a Christian. You meet a Christian you arrested before. What will you say to the Christian now? What will this Christian say back to you?

Paul says, "_____
_____."

The Christian says, "_____
_____."

Understanding the Word of God

Pretend that you are one of the people who traveled with Saul to Damascus. You saw what happened along the road. What do you feel? What do you say? What do you wonder about?

Saul's Conversion

The New Testament tells us that Saul persecuted, or hurt, Jesus' followers. When he did this, he persecuted Jesus. How can this be true?

Jesus and his followers are one. When we hurt one another, we hurt the Body of Christ, the members of the Church. This is an important truth that Saul learned on his way to Damascus.

After seeing the blinding light, the companions of Saul led him into Damascus. In Jerusalem his mind and heart had been blind. He could not love Christians. He could not understand them.

Paul's Faith

On the road to Damascus, Saul's mind and heart began to see. Jesus invited him to come out of his darkness and believe.

Faith Focus

How did Paul spread the good news of the Risen Jesus?

That is how faith is. It is like a seed planted in the dark ground. The seed grows up through the darkness. Suddenly, a new plant breaks through the crust of ground and sees the sun. The sun's light calls the seed to change and grow.

Jesus, the Son of God, called Saul to change and grow. Saul came to believe that God had raised Jesus to new life. And so Paul began to tell everyone the good news of God's love. Paul's heart had turned, or converted, to Jesus. This conversion changed his whole life.

To Help You Remember

1. What does the story about Saul's conversion teach you about Jesus?

2. What does the story teach you about faith?

Preach the Good News

Once more imagine that you are the apostle Paul. You are visiting a town to tell people about Jesus. On the scroll write what you think Paul says to the people in this town.

_____

_____

_____

How can you follow Paul's message?

_____

_____

_____

After his conversion, Paul began to tell everyone about Jesus. Like Paul, many Christians have preached the good news of Jesus' death and Resurrection. They became missionaries.

Saint John Neumann

One of these missionaries was John Neumann. Almost 200 years ago, he left his home in Europe. He sailed to the United States and became a priest in New York.

Father John Neumann traveled to the wilderness of New York State to tell others about Jesus. He also traveled to Maryland, Virginia, Pennsylvania, and Ohio.

When he was 41 years old, Father John became the bishop of Philadelphia. He organized the Catholic schools there and invited sisters to come and teach in these schools. Like Bishop Neumann, they shared the good news about Jesus with many children.

What part of the life of missionaries interests you the most?

Saint Paul and Saint John Neumann told others all about Jesus. You do this too in many ways. Through what you say and do, other people come to know Jesus and God's love for them.

God's Good News

Complete the chart to discover who hears about God's love from you.

I bring the good news of God's love to my family when I _____ .

I bring the good news of God's love to my friends when I _____ .

I bring the good news of God's love to my school when I _____ .

I bring the good news of God's love to my neighborhood when I _____ .

I bring the good news of God's love to _____ when I _____ .

My Faith Choice

This week I will try to share my faith in Jesus with others. I will try to

_____ .

And now we pray.

I will praise you, LORD, with all my heart; I will declare all your wondrous deeds.

Psalm 9:2

107

Match the words in column A with their definitions in column B.

Column A

_____ 1. Saul

_____ 2. Jerusalem

_____ 3. Pharisee

_____ 4. Ananias

_____ 5. conversion

_____ 6. Paul

Column B

a. Turning your heart from one thing to another

b. The place where Saul studied

c. What Saul became when he grew up

d. The name Saul took after his conversion

e. The man Jesus called on the road to Damascus

f. The man who healed Saul's blindness

Answer the following question.

What is the Good News that Paul preached?

_____

_____

_____

_____

Think and share with your family.

With your family, talk about your day. Share when and where each of you preached the Good News by your words and by your actions.

Visit our web site at www.FaithFirst.com

HERE WAS A MARRIAGE
IN CANA

Parent Page—Unit 2: We Worship

Your Role

The sacraments are some of the most wonderful times that we celebrate as Catholics. Baptisms, Confirmations, First Communions, weddings, and ordinations are usually times of great joy and excitement for our families. They are times of closeness when we feel the presence of God with us in a special way. They draw us closer to God and to one another. We also experience the presence of God in Reconciliation and in Anointing of the Sick. We feel God's help, strength, and forgiveness as we celebrate these sacraments. All the sacraments are concrete signs of God's presence and continuing action in our lives.

What We're Teaching

In this unit we deepen the children's understanding of the sacraments. As each sacrament is presented, we help the child to understand that the sacraments are not just events to celebrate. They are moments of God working in our lives. The Scripture story of Jesus washing the feet of his apostles provides a moving example of how we are to live as Christians. The story of the Pharisee and the tax collector helps your child understand that it is what is in our hearts that really counts.

Visit our web site at www.FaithFirst.com

What Difference Does It Make?

In every lesson of *Faith First,* the emphasis is not just on head learning, but also on transformation of the heart. Our faith is not just about knowing; it is about doing. Jesus no longer walks in our world, speaking to people and helping them in the same way he did while he lived on earth. He has passed this responsibility to us, as his followers. The sacraments not only strengthen us in our faith, but they also strengthen us in our mission as Christians. In these lessons on the sacraments, help your child translate the call to be Christian into concrete actions. You will find that the Scripture lessons contained in this unit can provide wonderful opportunities to talk to your child about living a life of faith.

Unit Opener Photographs: (top left) stained-glass window of the wedding feast at Cana; (top right) the butterfly is a sign of the Resurrection; (bottom) priest and children celebrating the communal rite of Reconciliation.

Celebrations of God's Love

We Pray

Father,
you give us grace
through sacramental
signs, which tell us
of the wonders of
your unseen power.

*The Rite of Baptism,
Blessing of the Water*

The sacraments are signs of God's love for us. What sacraments have you received? When did you receive them?

The sacrament of Baptism is the first sacrament we receive.

Faith Focus

What are the seven sacraments?

Faith Vocabulary

sacraments
Sacraments are the seven special celebrations that make Jesus present to us in a special way and make us sharers in God's life and love.

Jesus Gives Us the Sacraments

Our church family enjoys celebrating. Together we celebrate seven special **sacraments** given to us by Jesus.

Jesus gave us the sacraments as signs of God's love for us. When we celebrate the sacraments, we share in the life of the Holy Trinity. God the Father calls us to give praise and thanksgiving. Jesus helps us to bring God's good news of love to others. The Spirit helps us to become more like Jesus.

The Seven Sacraments

Confirmation strengthens in us the gifts of the Holy Spirit.

Baptism is the first sacrament we celebrate. Baptism makes us members of the Church and followers of Jesus. We receive the Holy Spirit and our sins are forgiven when we celebrate Baptism.

Eucharist is the sacrament in which we receive the Body and Blood of Christ. We are nourished and strengthened when we celebrate Eucharist.

Matrimony celebrates the lifelong love between a baptized man and a baptized woman.

To Help You Remember

1. Why did Jesus give us the sacraments?

2. How do the seven sacraments help us share in the life of the Trinity?

Holy Orders enables a man to serve the church community as a sign of Jesus at work among people.

Reconciliation celebrates God's forgiveness and mercy. Our sins are forgiven and we are given a new start in following Jesus.

Anointing of the Sick brings the healing and forgiveness of Jesus to those who are ill or elderly.

The Seven Sacraments

Look carefully at the pictures of the seven sacraments. Talk about the sacraments you have received or celebrated with others.

113

Faith Vocabulary

faith

Faith is both a gift from God that helps us to believe and trust in him and our response to that gift.

Celebrating Our Faith

Life is often a mystery. It takes **faith** to believe in many things that cannot be explained. The sacraments build on the faith we already have in God. Our faith grows stronger when we celebrate the sacraments.

Doubting Thomas

Faith did not come easy to one of Jesus' apostles. His name was Thomas. When the Risen Jesus first appeared to his followers, Thomas was not with them. Later the disciples told Thomas that God had raised Jesus to new life. Thomas refused to believe their words.

THOMAS: I must put my finger into the wounds in his hands. I must put my hand into the wound in his side. Only then will I believe.

(A week later the disciples are again gathered together. Thomas is with them. Suddenly, Jesus appears.)

JESUS: Peace be with you!

(turning to Thomas)

Put your finger into the nail marks in my hands. Put your hand into the wound in my side. Stop your doubting, Thomas, and believe!

THOMAS: My Lord and my God!

JESUS: Blessed are those who do not see me and yet believe.

Based on John 20:24–28

Seeing the nail marks, Thomas believed. Like Thomas, we also believe that God raised Jesus from death to life.

What Is Faith?

God shows himself to us in many ways. Although we cannot see God in the same way we see one another, we can recognize God's love in our lives.

We respond to God's love in faith. Faith is the gift from God that helps us trust that God is always with us. When we celebrate the sacraments, we express our faith in Jesus and all that God has done for us. When we celebrate the sacraments, we celebrate our faith in God's great love for us.

To Help You Remember

1. Which apostle was not with the disciples when the Risen Jesus appeared to them?

2. What do Jesus' words to Thomas tell us about the importance of faith?

The Gift of Faith

Complete the faith statement in each gift bag.

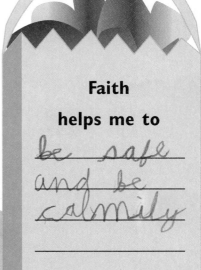

Faith helps me to
be safe and be calmily

Faith helps me to see God in
when I am hurt

Faith helps me to hear God when
I am in trobale

The Sacraments Touch Our Lives

Throughout our lives we change and grow. We grow and change in our faith life too. From birth to death the seven sacraments touch us at all the important moments of our lives.

Our parents' love gives us life. We are born into our family. Through Baptism we are born into the church family.

As we grow, our bodies grow stronger and stronger. Through Confirmation the Holy Spirit makes us stronger followers of Jesus.

As we grow, we share meals with friends and family. This food nourishes us and makes our bodies strong. As we grow, we prepare to join our church family at the table of the Lord to celebrate the Eucharist. The Body and Blood of Jesus nourishes our faith and makes us strong to live our faith.

With My Family

With your family, prepare a calendar to help you remember the days on which family members were baptized, confirmed, and received First Eucharist. Do something special together on these days.

As we grow, we learn that we can hurt others with our words and actions. We say we are sorry and try to do better. We celebrate the sacrament of Reconciliation as a way of saying we are sorry and want to do better.

To Help You Remember

1. How do the sacraments touch our lives?

2. Why are the seven sacraments celebrated throughout our lives?

When we are ill, our family members take care of us. Our church family also takes care of us through the sacrament of Anointing of the Sick. Through this sacrament the Church prays for us, and we are anointed with soothing oil.

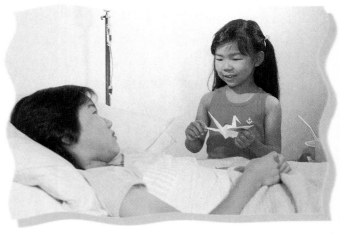

Many adults will marry. The Church blesses this commitment made by a man and a woman through the sacrament of Matrimony. Through their marriage a couple is a sign of God's love in the world.

God calls each of us to use our talents and skills to help other people. Through the sacrament of Holy Orders the Church blesses men who are called by God to serve the church family as deacons, priests, and bishops.

Special Sacraments

On these pages circle the sacraments that you have received. Underline the ones you have seen other people receive.

The sacraments have been given to us by Jesus. Celebrating the sacraments enables us to share in God's life and love.

Sacramentals

The Church also uses sacramentals to help us grow closer to God. Sacramentals are objects and blessings that we use in our worship and prayer. Some examples of sacramentals are holy water, the crucifix, and blessed religious medals.

The ashes we receive on our foreheads on Ash Wednesday and the holy oil used in celebrating some of the sacraments are also sacramentals.

Sacramentals help us remember that God is always with us. They deepen our faith in God's love for us.

Which of these sacramentals have you seen used in your parish church?

By celebrating the sacraments you grow closer to God the Father, Jesus, and the Holy Spirit.

Living the Sacraments

Write a letter to a friend telling about the sacraments you have received. Explain how these sacraments help you live as a follower of Jesus.

_____

_____

_____

_____

_____

My Faith Choice

To show that I am already a follower of Jesus, I will say to someone _____

_____ .

To show that I am trying to be a better follower of Jesus, I will _____

_____ .

And now we pray.

"My Lord and my God!"
John 20:28

Make each of the following sentences true
by changing the boldfaced word.

1. When we believe that God is with us and we
recognize his love in our lives, we have **penance.**

_____

2. The sacrament that celebrates our new birth in
Christ and the Church is **Matrimony.**

_____

3. The seven special celebrations of the Church that
make Jesus present are called **sacramentals.**

_____

4. The sacrament in which a man and a woman promise
to love each other for life is called **Confirmation.**

_____

Complete the sentences.

1. _____ was the apostle who had a difficult

time believing in Jesus' Resurrection.

2. _____ gave us the seven sacraments.

3. _____ are objects and

blessings the Church uses to help us grow closer to God.

Think and share with your family.
How does our faith in God help
us live each day?

Visit our
web site at
www.FaithFirst.com

We Celebrate God's Healing Love

We Pray

Lord, have mercy.
Christ, have mercy.
Lord, have mercy.

Jesus' words and actions tell us about God's healing love. We celebrate God's healing love in the sacraments of Reconciliation and Anointing of the Sick. What have you learned about these two sacraments?

Celebrating the Communal Rite of Reconciliation.

121

God, Our Forgiving Father

Stained-glass window of the loving father and prodigal son.

Faith Focus

What does God do for us when we say we are sorry for our sins?

Faith Vocabulary

forgive
> To pardon someone for the wrong they have done is to forgive.

With My Family

Talk about forgiveness. Retell a forgiveness story that took place in your family.

Sometimes everything seems to be going just right. You feel happy inside and your words and actions show it. But other times you might feel that everything is going wrong. You may have made some bad choices and you do not feel very good inside. This is when it is important to remember what forgiveness is all about.

God Always Forgives Us

Jesus once told a story about a father and a son. The son had done something wrong and wanted to be forgiven. The father wanted to **forgive** his son, if only the son would come home. Here is the wonderful story Jesus told.

A man had two sons. The younger son said to his father, "Give me my share of the family goods." So the father divided his goods between his two sons.

The younger son left home and went to a country far away. Soon he spent all his money. He did not even have any money left to buy food. The son was very hungry and sorry for what he had done. He decided to return home and ask for his father's forgiveness.

When he did, his father met him with open arms. The son said he was sorry for all he had done. The father forgave him and welcomed him home.

Based on Luke 15:11–24

To Help You Remember

1. Why did the son in the story need to ask for forgiveness?

2. How does this story help us understand God's forgiveness?

This story reminds us that God is our loving Father. God will always forgive us when we are sorry for our sins.

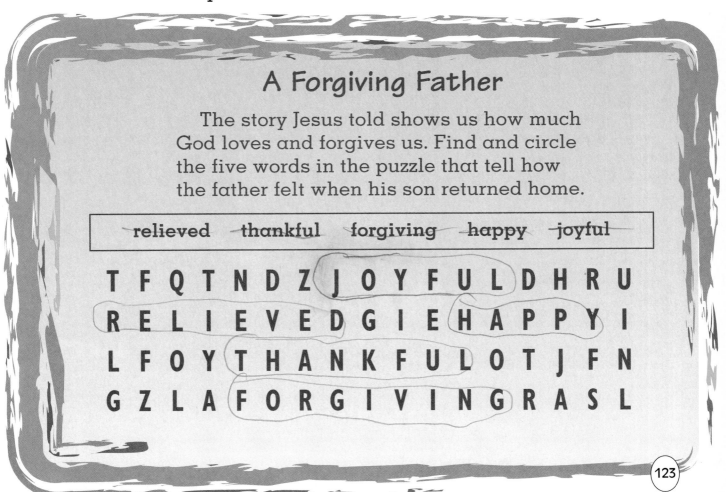

A Forgiving Father

The story Jesus told shows us how much God loves and forgives us. Find and circle the five words in the puzzle that tell how the father felt when his son returned home.

| relieved | thankful | forgiving | happy | joyful |

T F Q T N D Z J O Y F U L D H R U
R E L I E V E D G I E H A P P Y I
L F O Y T H A N K F U L O T J F N
G Z L A F O R G I V I N G R A S L

123

KIDS!! DO NOT EAT!!! THEY ARE FOR PICNIC.

Every day we make choices. Most of the time our choices are very good, but sometimes our choices are not the best choices. Sometimes we freely choose to do what we know is wrong.

When we freely choose to say or do something that is against God's law, we **sin.** We can also sin when we choose not to do something that we know we should do.

Jesus Forgives Us

When we sin, we ignore what God wants. We are selfish. We only think about ourselves. We do not think about the feelings and needs of others. Sin hurts our friendship with God and with other people.

Because God loves us, he sent Jesus to be our Savior. Jesus saves us from our sins so we can live with him in heaven.

Faith Focus

What happens when we sin?

Faith Vocabulary

sin

Freely choosing to do or say something that we know is against God's law is called sin.

When we are truly sorry for our sins and ask God for forgiveness, he forgives us. God heals us with his grace. The Holy Spirit helps us not to sin again. We are reconciled, or made friends again, with God and the members of the Church.

Thanking Jesus

Write a prayer to Jesus. Thank him for being our Savior and for forgiving our sins.

thank you Jesus!

Faith Focus

Why do we celebrate the sacraments of Reconciliation and Anointing of the Sick?

Faith Vocabulary

Reconciliation

Reconciliation is the sacrament that celebrates God's forgiveness and mercy. This sacrament is also called the sacrament of Penance.

penance

A penance is a prayer or good deed that is given to us by the priest in the sacrament of Reconciliation.

contrition

Contrition is the sorrow we feel when we have done something wrong.

We receive God's healing love when we celebrate the sacrament of **Reconciliation.** In this sacrament we show God we are sorry for our sins. We ask for and receive God's forgiveness.

The Sacrament of Reconciliation

We celebrate the sacrament of Reconciliation this way.

1. We examine our conscience. We think about the loving and unloving choices we have made.
2. The priest welcomes us. We listen to a reading from the Bible about God's healing love.
3. We confess our sins to the priest.
4. The priest talks about how we can make better choices. He gives us a **penance.**
5. We tell God that we are sorry. We pray a prayer of sorrow, or act of **contrition.**

6. The priest prays the prayer of absolution. This is the prayer of our forgiveness. Our sins are forgiven by the power of the Holy Spirit.

Anointing of the Sick

Jesus often healed the sick during his life on earth. Christ's work among the sick continues in the world today through the Church. This work continues in a special way through the sacrament of Anointing of the Sick.

The priest visits members of the Church who are seriously ill, weak because of their old age, or in danger of dying. He anoints their hands and forehead with a special oil. This sacrament brings us strength and courage and peace in our sickness.

To Help You Remember

1. What do we do when we celebrate the sacrament of Reconciliation?

2. Why do we celebrate the sacrament of Anointing of the Sick?

Understanding the Sacrament of Reconciliation

Write 1 before words the priest would say and 2 before words you might say while celebrating the sacrament of Reconciliation.

_2_ "I'm sorry."

_2_ "I want to do better."

_1_ "I absolve you from your sins."

_2_ "I was mean to my little brother."

_1_ "For your penance, do something kind this week for your brother."

_1_ "Go in peace."

127

Jesus gave us the sacrament of Reconciliation. Through Reconciliation we receive and celebrate God's loving forgiveness.

The Pope Forgives

Christians thank God for the gift of forgiveness by forgiving others. On May 13, 1981, in Saint Peter's Square in Rome, Italy, a large crowd was cheering for Pope John Paul II. Two shots were fired. The bullets hit the pope's arm, hand, and stomach.

Police quickly arrested Mehmet Ali Agca, a terrorist, and took him to jail. They rushed the pope to the hospital. It took five hours for doctors to save his life. Days later people around the world wanted justice and punishment.

The pope said, "Pray for the brother who shot me, whom I have sincerely forgiven."

Two years later Pope John Paul II visited Agca in prison. They talked privately for twenty minutes. When the visit was over, Agca leaned over and kissed the hand of the man he tried to kill. Agca knew what it meant to be forgiven. Pope John Paul II forgave his enemy as Jesus taught us to do.

What does this story teach you about forgiveness?

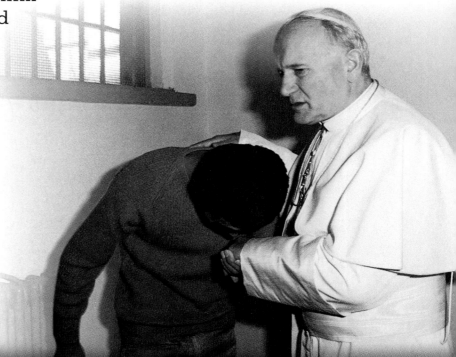

Asking and receiving forgiveness is an important part of your life. Knowing that God forgives you when you say you are sorry helps you grow into a more loving person.

Forgiveness Words

Put a 1 next to the words you could use to ask forgiveness. Put a 2 next to the words you could use to forgive someone else.

__1__ I'm sorry.

__2__ You are forgiven.

__2__ That's okay.

__1__ I'll try not to do that again.

__2__ We're still friends.

__1__ Can we still be friends?

__1__ I know I was wrong to do that.

My Faith Choice

This week I will show that forgiveness is important in my life by speaking these words,

_____

_____ , and by doing this action,

_____ .

And now we pray.

Lord, have mercy.
Christ, have mercy.
Lord, have mercy.

Match the words in column A with their meanings in column B.

Column A

___a___ 1. sin

___e___ 2. contrition

___b___ 3. sacrament of Reconciliation

___c___ 4. penance

___d___ 5. absolution

Column B

a. Freely choosing to do what we know is against God's law

b. A special way the Church has of celebrating God's forgiveness and mercy

c. Something we do to show that we want to make up for our sins

d. A prayer the priest prays that tells us that we are forgiven

e. The sorrow we feel when we do something we know is wrong

Complete the sentences.

1. God wants to _forgive_ us when we are sorry.

2. God sent Jesus to be our _savior_ .

3. Before celebrating the sacrament of Reconciliation, we examine our _consci_ .

4. Through the Church the priest _absolves_ us from our sins.

5. A _penance_ is a prayer we pray or a kind act we do to show that we are really sorry for our sins.

Think and share with your family.

Talk with your family about why you think Jesus spent so much time telling stories of God's forgiving love.

Visit our web site at www.FaithFirst.com

The Pharisee and the Tax Collector

A Scripture Story

13

We Pray

God our Father,
we know that
you are good.
You love us and do
great things for us.

*From Eucharistic Prayer
for Masses with Children I*

There are many
stories in the Gospel
about forgiveness.
You have heard some
of these stories many
times. What do you
remember about
what the Gospel
teaches about
forgiveness?

*Stained-glass window
showing Jesus' parable
of the Pharisee and the
tax collector.*

Model of the Temple in the time of Jesus.

We know about many kinds of responsibilities and jobs people have. There are presidents and senators, mail carriers and tax collectors, priests and bishops. Each of these people has a different job to do.

Faith Focus

What were some differences between the Pharisees and publicans?

Faith Vocabulary

The Temple

The place in Jerusalem where the Jewish people worshiped God is called the Temple.

Pharisees

In Jesus' time, Pharisees were religious leaders of the Jewish people. They followed the Law of Moses very closely. For example, on Mondays and Thursdays Pharisees ate no food. They also refused to drink water.

Tax Collectors

In Jesus' time, tax collectors were also called publicans. Some of them collected more taxes than people owed. They kept the extra money for themselves.

Because of this, many people thought that tax collectors were sinners. The Jewish people thought that many tax collectors were dishonest and greedy, and they stayed away from them.

Temple Prayer

Both Pharisees and tax collectors prayed at the **Temple** in Jerusalem. They often spoke their prayers aloud. Sometimes they held their hands up, reaching toward heaven. Sometimes they beat their chest with their fist. This showed that they were sorry for their sins and needed God's mercy and forgiveness.

Sometimes they prayed kneeling or sitting or standing. They also prayed by bowing to God. This showed their respect for God.

To Help You Remember

1. What is a Pharisee?

2. Why did the Jewish people think that tax collectors were sinners?

Praying

What are some gestures or positions we use when we pray?

we kneel stand sit bow and fold our hands

What is your favorite way to pray?

standing

Faith Focus

Which man in the parable truly depended on God?

Faith Vocabulary

parable

A parable is a story that helped people understand and live what Jesus was teaching.

Most of us like people who do not brag about themselves. We like humble people. Humble people know that all their gifts come from God.

Jesus Tells a Parable

One day Jesus told a **parable,** or story, about a Pharisee and a tax collector. He told the story to a group of people gathered around him. These people believed that they were better than other people. They believed that God thought they were better too. This is the story Jesus told.

Two men went into the Temple to pray. One was a Pharisee. The other was a tax collector.

The Pharisee stood in the center of the Temple and prayed. "Thank you, God, that I am not like other people. I am not greedy or dishonest. Thank you that I am not like that tax collector over there. I fast twice a week. I give one-tenth of my income to the Temple."

The tax collector stood toward the back of the Temple. He did not even raise his eyes. He knew he was a sinner. He beat his chest and said, "God, forgive me, for I am a sinner."

Jesus then told his listeners what the parable meant. He said that God forgave the sins of the tax collector. The tax collector went home at peace with himself and with God.

Based on Luke 18:9–14

To Help You Remember

1. To whom did Jesus tell this parable?

2. Explain what the Pharisee did and said.

Jesus told this parable to help us understand that we all need God's forgiveness.

Remembering the Parable

In the puzzle circle the eight terms that will help you to remember this story about being humble.

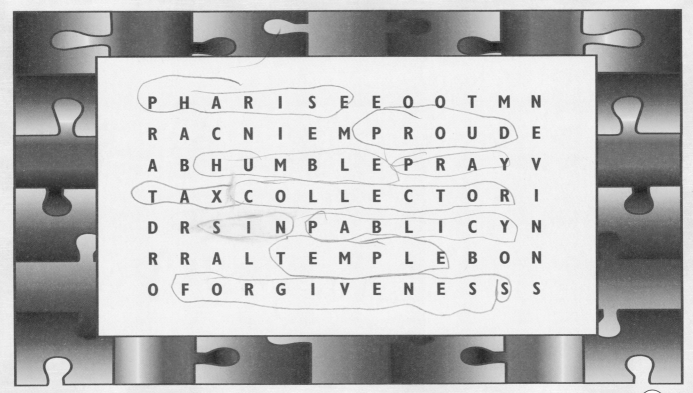

P H A R I S E E O O T M N
R A C N I E M P R O U D E
A B H U M B L E P R A Y V
T A X C O L L E C T O R I
D R S I N P A B L I C Y N
R R A L T E M P L E B O N
O F O R G I V E N E S S S

135

Understanding the Word of God

Faith Focus

Why did Jesus tell this parable?

Faith Vocabulary

humble

Humble means being aware that God is the giver of all gifts and that we are all equal in God's sight.

With My Family

Ask someone in your family to tell you another parable that Jesus told. Then find the parable in the Bible. Read it together and listen for Jesus' message. Share what the parable means to each of you.

When Jesus told the parable of the Pharisee and the tax collector, many people listened. How do you think they felt about what Jesus said? How would you have felt if you had been standing close to Jesus?

God Forgives the Humble

Jesus told this parable to proud people who thought they did not need God's forgiveness.

In the parable the Pharisee believes that he lives a holy life. He believes that he has made himself holy. He does not need God or God's forgiveness. The Pharisee does not understand that God helps him to do all he does.

Jesus wants the crowd of people to understand that God wants people to be **humble.** The tax collector in the parable is humble. He knows that he has sinned. He admits he needs God's forgiveness. In deep sorrow, he begs God to hear the prayer of a sinner.

136

We Need Forgiveness

Jesus told this story to help all of us understand that we all depend on God. Everyone is to be humble before God. God is the Creator. We are God's children. All our talents are gifts from God. We did not create ourselves. God created us. So we humbly thank God for his great goodness to us.

In the Old Testament we read the following,

> Do what is right, love goodness, and walk humbly with your God.
>
> Based on Micah 6:8

These are words we all are called to follow.

To Help You Remember

1. How did the tax collector act in this story?

2. What was Jesus teaching by telling the story of the Pharisee and the tax collector?

Parables Teach Us

Write a four-line poem or song that tells what you learned from the parable of the Pharisee and the tax collector.

_____

_____

_____

_____

Jesus told parables to teach us how to live. The parable of the Pharisee and the tax collector teaches us to be humble. It teaches us to depend on God.

Saint Augustine

Many saints have learned to be humble and depend on God. When he was young, Augustine was proud. He felt no need for God. He refused to pray or ask for God's forgiveness.

One day God spoke to Augustine and the young man listened. In his heart he heard God's words. He heard God invite him to change and be humble.

Augustine learned to depend on God. For the rest of his life, he prayed often and asked for forgiveness. God asked him to change. Augustine prayed, and the Holy Spirit helped him to change. And as he changed, he became a happy man.

What does Saint Augustine teach us about being humble?

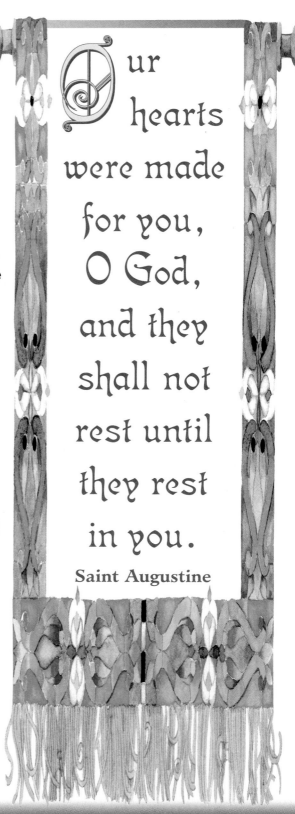

Our hearts were made for you, O God, and they shall not rest until they rest in you.

Saint Augustine

What Difference Does It Make in My Life?

Each year you are growing in your love of God. You are learning what a difference it makes to recognize and trust in God's goodness and great love for you.

Picture This

In each section of film, draw a picture of yourself showing love for God and others. Draw something that you did yesterday that was right.

Draw what good thing you did or will do today for someone else.

Draw what you will do tomorrow to show you recognize God's love for you.

Yesterday

Today

Tomorrow

My Faith Choice

Check something you can do this week to show God that you depend on him.

_____ I can remember that God is always with me.

_____ I can ask God's help when I need it.

And now we pray.

LORD, my God, in you I place my trust.
Based on Psalm 25:1

139

CHAPTER REVIEW

Circle *T* (true) or *F* (false) for each sentence.

1. The Pharisee was a very humble man.   T   F

2. The tax collector told God in prayer that he was glad he was not like the Pharisee.   T   F

3. The Pharisee did not depend on God.   T   F

4. Jesus teaches us that we all need God's love and forgiveness.   T   F

5. Jesus often used parables to teach.   T   F

Answer the following questions.

1. To whom does Jesus tell the story of the Pharisee and the tax collector?

_____

_____

2. What does Jesus want us to learn from this story?

_____

_____

3. In what ways does Jesus want us to be like the tax collector?

_____

_____

Think and share with your family.

Memorize Micah 6:8, which is on page 137. Pray this verse with your family at night before you go to bed.

Visit our web site at www.FaithFirst.com

The Sacraments of Service

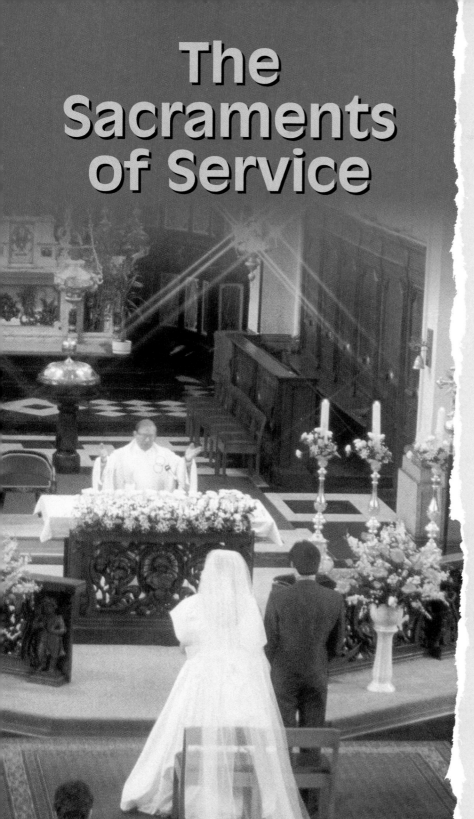

14

We Pray

Father,
in your plan for
salvation you
provide shepherds
for your people.
Fill your Church
with the spirit of
courage and love.

*Opening Prayer from the
Mass for Priestly Vocations*

God calls some
members of the
Church to serve all
the members of the
Church as bishops,
priests, deacons, and
married people. What
are the names of the
two sacraments that
celebrate these
special callings?

*Christian married
couples are signs of
Christ's love for the
Church.*

141

Faith Focus

What is our vocation as Christians?

Faith Vocabulary

vocation

Our call from God to share in Jesus' life and work is called our vocation. We live this call in many ways.

Sometimes someone who is important to us tells us something that we never forget. And sometimes someone we love does something so special for us that we always remember how it made us feel. Share about a time when this may have happened to you.

Jesus Teaches Us to Serve

At the Last Supper Jesus did something for his apostles that they never forgot. By doing this he taught them a very important lesson. The lesson is for all Jesus' friends and followers. So it is for us too.

On the night before he died, Jesus ate a last meal with his friends. During the meal he got up from the table. He picked up a towel and a bowl.

Jesus poured water into the bowl and began to wash his disciples' feet. He dried their feet with the towel.

Peter did not want Jesus to wash his feet because Jesus was Peter's teacher and master. But Jesus said that he wanted to do this for his followers. He wanted to serve them.

Afterward Jesus said, "You call me your teacher and your master. Yet I have washed your feet. If I, the teacher and master, do this, so should you. I have given you an example. Do what I have done."

Based on John 13:1–17

By washing the feet of his followers, Jesus calls us to serve others as he did. God calls each of us to share in Jesus' life and work. We call that our **vocation.** As Catholics we are called to serve one another in many ways.

To Help You Remember

1. What did Jesus ask his followers to do?

2. Why did Jesus wash his disciples' feet?

We Serve Others

Think about this list of ways you can serve others. Then check one and write how you can put it into action this week.

I can serve others by

_____ being patient and kind.

_____ sharing with others.

_____ telling the truth.

_____ helping my family.

_____ playing fairly.

_____

_____

_____

Faith Focus

How do bishops, priests, and deacons serve the People of God?

Faith Vocabulary

Sacraments at the Service of Communion
The sacraments of Matrimony and Holy Orders are known as the Sacraments at the Service of Communion.

Holy Orders
Holy Orders is the sacrament that celebrates the ordaining of a man as a bishop, a priest, or a deacon to serve the People of God in the name of Jesus.

Bishop ordaining a deacon.

God calls some members of the Church to serve all the People of God in special ways. These special callings are celebrated in the **Sacraments at the Service of Communion.** One of those sacraments is called **Holy Orders.** The other is called the sacrament of Matrimony.

The Sacrament of Holy Orders

Bishops, priests, and deacons have served the Church from the days of the apostles. They are called to serve the whole Church, the People of God, in the sacrament of **Holy Orders.** The sacrament of Holy Orders lasts forever.

Through Holy Orders a man becomes a priest. He is a priest forever. He serves the people of the Church in Jesus' name. He lives his life unmarried. This helps him serve the People of God in a fuller way.

Some priests are pastors, or leaders, of a parish family. Other priests serve parishes as helpers to the pastor. And still others serve God's people as teachers and missionaries and in many other ways. They also serve God's people by presiding over the Eucharist and other sacraments.

Deacons are not priests. They are ordained by a bishop to serve the Church in many ways. Deacons proclaim the Good News of the Gospel at Mass. They can also baptize new members of the Catholic community. They can lead the celebration of the sacrament of Matrimony. They especially care for the poor and the sick.

Bishops serve the People of God in a very special way. They take the place of the apostles in the Church today. Jesus leads the Church today through the pope and the bishops. The pope is the leader of the whole Church. Other bishops are in charge of dioceses. Only bishops can ordain other bishops, priests, and deacons. They lead the people in worshiping God. They teach people about the Gospel and God's love for them. One way bishops teach is by writing letters that guide us in living as Catholics.

To Help You Remember

1. Who is called to serve in the sacrament of Holy Orders?

2. How do bishops, priests, and deacons serve God's people?

Serving the People of God

Write the word *Bishop*, *Priest*, or *Deacon* after the sentences that best describe who is serving the Church.

- Sometimes I read the Gospel at Mass. _____
- I preside over the Eucharist. _____
- I am the leader of a diocese. _____
- I can ordain priests, bishops and deacons through the sacrament of Holy Orders. _____
- I am sometimes a pastor of a parish. _____
- I can witness at the celebration of Matrimony. _____

The Sacrament of Matrimony

Matrimony is also a Sacrament at the Service of Communion. Through this sacrament, God calls a baptized man and a baptized woman to serve the Church, the People of God, as a married couple.

Faith Focus

How do married people serve the People of God?

Faith Vocabulary

Matrimony
  Matrimony is the sacrament that unites a baptized man and a baptized woman forever in love as husband and wife.

In Matrimony a man and a woman freely make lifelong promises. They promise to always be faithful to each other. They promise to care for one another and to treat each other with honor and respect.

The Holy Spirit helps husbands and wives to love one another just as Jesus loves his Church. They serve the Church by raising children to be followers of Christ. In this way they are signs of God's love in the world.

Following God's Call

At your Baptism, you were called to live as a follower of Christ. When you grow up, you will make a decision about how you will follow Christ as an adult.

Many of you will decide to get married. Some of you may become deacons, priests, or religious brothers or sisters. Some of you will remain single.

No matter what you do, you will always be called to live as a faithful and loyal follower of Christ. Sometimes that will be easy to do. Sometimes it may be difficult to do. But this is for certain. The Holy Spirit will always be with you to help you.

To Help You Remember

1. What do a man and a woman promise in the sacrament of Matrimony?

2. How do husbands and wives serve the Church?

With My Family

Talk about how the members of your family take care of one another and serve one another.

Following Jesus

Write a prayer asking the Holy Spirit to help you know what God wants you to do with your life. Say this prayer often.

_____

_____

_____

_____

_____

_____

Jesus calls everyone who is baptized to serve others. Through the sacraments of Holy Orders and Matrimony, members of our Church are called to serve the whole Church as priests, deacons, bishops, or as married couples.

Deacons Serve the Church

Many parishes have deacons. Perhaps your parish does. You may have asked: What is a deacon? Frequently, the deacon is married and has a family. He might be a teacher or a construction worker. He might have young children or he might be a grandfather.

After proper training deacons are ordained by a bishop. They are called permanent deacons. They serve the Church in many ways under the authority of their bishop. They assist at worship. They proclaim and preach the Word of God. They minister the sacrament of Baptism. They serve the people by visiting and praying with people who are sick. They also serve people who are in need of food, clothing, or a home. Deacons serve people as Jesus taught his followers to serve people.

List the ways a deacon can help the people of your parish serve others.

You have been called by God to live as a follower of Jesus.

RESPECTFUL GENEROUS

CARING

LOVING

PATIENT KIND

Followers of Jesus

The words in the border describe someone who is a follower of Jesus. Choose one of these qualities and color in the letters. Tell how you live that quality.

_____

_____

_____

Then share how living that quality affects your family and friends.

_____

_____

_____

FORGIVING HONEST

My Faith Choice

The two words above that best describe me are _____ and _____ .

One word above that I would like to put into practice more often is

_____ .

And now we pray.

LORD, help me understand how you want me to live.
I will try with all my heart.
Based on Psalm 119:34

Match the words in column A with their definitions in column B.

Column A

___ 1. bishop

___ 2. deacon

___ 3. priest

Column B

a. Serves the Church as a teacher and a leader of a diocese

b. An ordained minister of the Church, who is not a priest, who is ordained to help the bishop in his work

c. Helps bishops by serving the people of a parish, presiding over the Eucharist, and in other ways

Fill in the blanks.

1. All Christians are called to live as a follower of Jesus at _____ .

2. In the sacrament of _____ _____, a baptized man is ordained a priest, bishop, or deacon.

3. In the sacrament of _____, a baptized man and a baptized woman are called to serve the Church as a married couple.

Think and share with your family.

With your family, discuss how the priest and deacon in your parish serve you as members of God's family. Then talk about how your family might help them.

Visit our web site at www.FaithFirst.com

The Wedding Feast at Cana

A Scripture Story

15

THERE WAS A MARRIAGE IN CANA

We Pray

God, strengthen the faith of this couple and through them, bless the Church. We ask this through Jesus, your Son. Amen.

Based on the Opening Prayer of the Wedding Mass

Through Jesus, God worked many miracles. What miracle stories in the Gospel do you know?

In the Gospel according to John, we read about Jesus' first miracle at the wedding feast in Cana.

Faith Focus

What was a Jewish wedding like in the time of Jesus?

With My Family

Find some pictures of a family get-together with friends and relatives. Talk with your family about the food and the fun. Talk about how your family would have felt if you had no food or drink to share.

Weddings make us happy! When a woman and a man marry, we celebrate. We laugh and dance and sing and eat! We wish the couple a good life, filled with love.

Jewish Weddings

During Jesus' time a Jewish wedding began in the evening. The bridegroom and his friends walked to the bride's home. The bride, wearing a veil, met them at the door. Her ten bridesmaids carried lighted lamps and stood next to her.

Then the wedding party walked back to the groom's home for the wedding ceremony. Along the way the village people sang songs and cheered and wished them well.

The next day the wedding party danced and sang and opened presents. For seven days the bridegroom and his family provided food and wine for all the guests. People came from far and near to celebrate the wedding.

Water and Wine

Many Jewish weddings took place in the fall of the year. The farmers had harvested their crops. The hard work was over and people wanted to celebrate. So when they came to a wedding, they came with happy hearts.

The bridegroom kept the wine used at the wedding in large stone, or pottery, jars. He also had other large jars filled with water. During the wedding, waiters would fill these jars with water from the well.

To Help You Remember

1. How long did a Jewish wedding feast last?

2. Why were the guests so happy to be at a wedding?

You Are Invited

Make an invitation inviting Jesus to a celebration you are having.

Reading the Word of God

Faith Focus

What happened to the water in the six stone jars?

Faith Vocabulary

Cana
Cana is a walled town about five miles from Nazareth where Jesus grew up.

Galilee
Galilee is a section of the land where Jesus lived and did the work God sent him to do while he was on earth.

Gospel according to John
The Gospel according to John is one of the first four books of the New Testament. The word *gospel* means "good news."

Jesus Helps a Newly Married Couple

Once Jesus, his mother, and the disciples went to a wedding at **Cana** in **Galilee**. The **Gospel according to John** tells what happened at the wedding. During the wedding, the groom's family ran out of wine. Mary saw that they had no wine.

MARY: Jesus, they have no wine.

JESUS: How can I help them, Mother?

MARY: *(to the waiters)*
Do whatever he tells you to do.

JESUS: *(to the waiters)*
Fill those six stone jars with water.

NARRATOR: The waiters fill the six jars with water from the well. Each jar holds twenty to thirty gallons of water.

JESUS: Take some of what is in the jars to the headwaiter.

NARRATOR: A waiter follows Jesus' command. The headwaiter tastes what is in the jars. Then he sends for the groom.

HEADWAITER: *(to the groom)* Usually people serve their best wine first. Then, when people do not notice anymore, they serve the cheaper wine. But you have kept the best for last!

Based on John 2:1–11

Jesus changed the water into wine at Cana in Galilee. Because of this sign, his disciples began to believe in him.

To Help You Remember

1. What did Jesus do at the wedding in Cana?

2. Why was the headwaiter surprised?

Write a Letter from Cana

Imagine that you are a waiter at the wedding in Cana. Write a letter to a friend who lives in Nazareth. Remember that this is the town where Jesus grew up. Tell your friend all that happened and explain what you now think about Jesus.

_____

_____

_____

_____

_____

_____

_____

_____

Understanding the Word of God

Faith Focus

What do miracles tell us about God?

Faith Vocabulary

miracle
  A miracle is a sign of God's power and presence with us.

In the story of the wedding feast at Cana, the wine ran out. Then Jesus told the waiters to draw water from the well and fill six jars. When the headwaiter tasted the water, it had become wine! He did not know where the wine had come from. Of course, the waiters knew. And so do you!

Jesus Works a Miracle

In changing the water into wine, Jesus performed a **miracle.** Miracles are signs that God works among us. They tell us that God invites us to believe in him.

Seeing this miracle of water changed into wine, Jesus' followers began to believe in him. They believed that he was sent to them by God.

The Healing of the Blind Beggar.
Luke 18:35—43

The Calming of a Storm at Sea.
Mark 4:35—41

156

God Is with Us

According to church teaching, a miracle is a sign of God's power at work in our world. The New Testament tells us that Jesus worked many miracles. It is a sign that God is with us. God is always loving us. People came to have faith and trust in God because of the miracles Jesus performed.

The Healing of a Paralyzed Man. Luke 5:17–20

To Help You Remember

1. What is a miracle?

2. What does the miracle of water changed into wine tell you about God?

Other Miracles and Signs

Choose one of the miracle stories pictured on these two pages. Read the story in the Bible and complete the sentences.

The miracle in this story is that _____

_____

_____.

This miracle tells me that God _____

_____

_____.

God worked miracles and wonders through Jesus. These were signs that helped people have faith and trust in God. Through the miracles that Jesus performed, God's power and love was at work in our world.

Signs of God's Love

Jesus did not only work miracles. He helped people in many other ways too. He fed the hungry and cared for the sick. He healed people's broken hearts and wounded dreams.

Ever since Jesus walked this earth, the Church has helped people. As members of the Church, we feed the hungry and care for the sick. We reach out to people who are lonely. We provide a bed for the homeless.

When we do these things, we are signs of God's love. We bring God's healing and comfort to people. We are signs of God's love for people.

What does your parish do that is a sign of God's love for people?

God is with you always. You are called to be a sign of God's love to others.

Signs of God's Love All Around Us

Complete these sentences to show your faith in God's love.

Each time I see a _____ ,
I see a sign of God's love.

Each time I hear a _____ ,
I hear a sign of God's love.

Each time I taste a _____ ,
I taste a sign of God's love.

Each time I feel a _____ ,
I feel a sign of God's love.

Each time I smell a _____ ,
I smell a sign of God's love.

My Faith Choice

This week I will look for God's love in

_____ .

This week I will listen for God's love in

_____ .

And now we pray.
Thank you, LORD, for all your goodness; your love lasts forever.
Based on Psalm 118:1

Match the words in column A with their definitions in column B.

Column A

_____ 1. miracle

_____ 2. Cana

_____ 3. Galilee

_____ 4. Gospel according to John

Column B

a. The place of the wedding feast where Jesus turned water into wine

b. A section of the land where Jesus lived and did the work God sent him to do

c. One of the first four books of the New Testament

d. A sign of God's power and presence with us

Answer the following questions.

1. What led Jesus to perform this miracle at Cana?

_____

2. How did the miracle help the disciples?

_____

3. What does a miracle tell us about God?

_____

Think and share with your family.

Talk with your family about the signs of God's power and presence in your lives. Make a poster about these "miracles." Display your poster in your house to remind you and your family of God's presence.

Visit our web site at www.FaithFirst.com

We Celebrate the Eucharist

16

We Pray

Father,
all-powerful and
ever-living God, we
do well always and
everywhere to give
you thanks through
Jesus Christ our Lord.
*Preface for Sundays
in Ordinary Time*

We celebrate the
Eucharist as a parish
community. We give
thanks and praise to
God for all God's
gifts, especially for
Jesus. What are some
of the important
things we say and
do at Mass?

*The bread and wine
we offer at Mass become
the Body and Blood of
Christ.*

We Give Thanks to God

Faith Focus

Why do we celebrate the Eucharist?

Faith Vocabulary

Eucharist

The Eucharist is the sacrament in which we receive the Body and Blood of Christ. The word *eucharist* means "to give thanks."

Think of a special meal you have eaten with your family in the last year. What kinds of foods did you eat? What family stories did you tell? What made this meal a real celebration?

Jesus Shares a Special Meal

Jesus and his friends and family shared many meals together. One meal, shared on the night before he died, was the most special meal of all. We call this meal the Last Supper, or the Lord's Supper. Read and discover what the Gospel according to Matthew tells us about that meal.

While they were eating, Jesus took bread. He prayed a special blessing prayer and broke the bread. Then he gave it to his disciples, saying, "Take and eat this. This is my body."

Then he took a cup of wine and gave thanks to his Father. Then he gave it to his disciples, saying, "Drink from it, all of you, for this is my blood."

Based on Matthew 26:26–28

When we celebrate the Eucharist, we do what Jesus did at the Last Supper. We come together to celebrate the gift of Jesus in the **Eucharist.** The Eucharist joins us more fully to Jesus and to one another.

To Help You Remember

1. What happened at the Last Supper?

2. When can you gather with your church family to celebrate the Eucharist?

Giving Thanks to God

You have many reasons to give thanks to God. Use the letters in the word *eucharist* to show your thanks to God. For each letter, think of someone or something that includes that letter and write it there.

E
U
C
H
TH**A**NKS
R
I
S
T

With My Family

Before you go to Mass next weekend, read the gospel reading for that Sunday. Talk about what the reading means for your family.

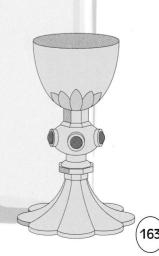

Faith Vocabulary

Mass
Mass is the celebration of listening to God's word and giving thanks and praise to God for the gift of Jesus.

Liturgy of the Word
The first part of the Mass, in which we listen and respond to God's word, is called the Liturgy of the Word.

Liturgy of the Eucharist
The second part of the Mass, in which we remember and take part in Jesus' life, death, and Resurrection, is called the Liturgy of the Eucharist.

We Give Thanks

God has filled our lives with gifts of his life and love. At **Mass** we thank God for all his gifts, especially for his greatest gift—Jesus.

At Mass we remember how much God loved us when he sent his own Son into our world. We remember how much Jesus loved us when he died on the cross for us and was raised to new life. We remember God's great love for us and give thanks and praise.

The word *eucharist* means "to give thanks." At the Eucharist we do what Jesus asked us to do. Together we share a meal of blessing and thanksgiving. We bless and give thanks to God.

During the first part of the Mass, we listen and respond to God's word. God speaks to us through the readings from Sacred Scripture. This part of the celebration is called the **Liturgy of the Word.**

The **Liturgy of the Eucharist** is the second part of the Mass. During this part of our celebration, we remember and take part in Jesus' life, death, and Resurrection. We join with Christ in offering himself to God.

The bread and wine become the Body and Blood of Christ. This "consecrated" bread and wine are truly and really the Body and Blood of Christ.

We receive the gift of the Body and Blood of Christ at Holy Communion. This joins us more closely with Jesus Christ and his Church.

To Help You Remember

1. What does the word *eucharist* mean?

2. Why do we thank God the Father at Mass?

Love and Serve the Lord

At the end of Mass the priest says, "Go in peace to love and serve the Lord." What are three ways you can love and serve the Lord this week?

At home I will ___do chores___

_____.

At school I will _____

_____.

In my neighborhood I will _____

_____.

Faith Vocabulary

tabernacle

A tabernacle is a special box in which the Blessed Sacrament is kept.

Blessed Sacrament

The Blessed Sacrament is the Eucharist that the Church keeps in the tabernacle to distribute to the sick and for private adoration.

The Blessed Sacrament

Our parish family cannot always eat together at the Lord's table. Some of us might be sick, in the hospital, or too old to come to church for Mass. Our parish family wants everyone to be able to receive Jesus in the Eucharist.

After Mass the Eucharist is brought to those in our parish family who are sick. The Church keeps consecrated eucharistic bread, or hosts, in the **tabernacle.** The Eucharist kept in the tabernacle is called the **Blessed Sacrament.** A special candle called the sanctuary lamp is kept burning nearby. This reminds us that Jesus is truly present with us in a special way in the Blessed Sacrament.

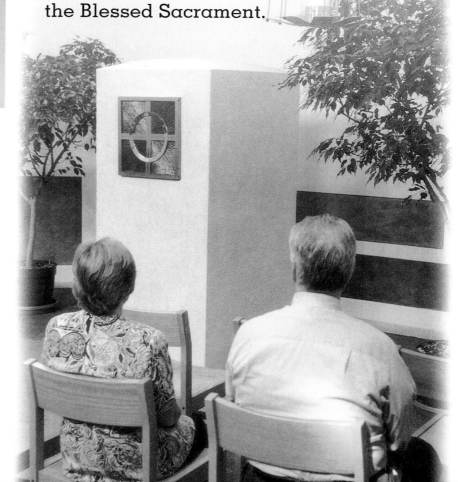

Jesus Is with Us Always

We can also adore or worship Jesus by spending time in prayer before the Blessed Sacrament. We thank God for Jesus' life, death, and Resurrection. We ask God to help us live as his children.

To Help You Remember

1. What is the Blessed Sacrament?

2. Why is the Blessed Sacrament kept in the tabernacle?

Jesus Is with Us

If you could design a tabernacle for your church, what would it look like? Draw it in the space provided. Be sure to include a sanctuary lamp in your picture.

The Eucharist is the center of the life of the Church. It is the center of our lives as Christians.

The Day of the Lord

Celebrating the Mass on Sunday has always had special meaning for the Church. Sunday is the first day of the week. Over the centuries, Christians have celebrated Sunday as "the day of the Lord" and "the day to break bread."

Eucharist gives meaning to every Sunday in our life. Sundays are meant to be different. Receiving the Eucharist joins us more closely to Jesus and to one another.

Going to Mass on Sunday reminds us that God wants us to start each week by giving praise and thanks to him.

What do you do on Sunday to make it a special day to thank and praise God?

Every time you take part in the celebration of Mass, Jesus is present with you in a special way. He is present with you in the Scripture. He is especially present in the Eucharist.

A Prayer of Thanksgiving

Write a prayer to Jesus. Thank him for being with you in so many ways, especially in the Eucharist.

_____

_____

_____

_____

_____

_____

My Faith Choice

When I go to Mass, I will remember Jesus is present with us. We join with him to give thanks and praise to God.

And now we pray.

Lord Jesus Christ, we worship you living among us in the sacrament of your body and blood.
Alternate Opening Prayer
The Body and Blood of Christ

Complete each sentence.

1. The _Last supper_ is the
   name we give to the meal Jesus shared with the
   disciples on the night before he died.

2. Through the power of the Holy Spirit, the bread
   and wine at Mass become the

   _____.

3. The two main parts of the Mass are
   the Liturgy of the _eucharist_
   and the Liturgy of the _word_.

4. We receive the gift of the Body and Blood of
   Christ at _The Liturgy of the eucharist._

Answer the following questions.

1. What did Jesus give us at the Last Supper?
   Jesus gave us bread and wine

2. What great prayer is the center of our lives as Christians?
   The great prayer

3. What is the meaning of the word *eucharist*?
   The meaning of the word eucharist is to "give thanks to."

Think and share with your family.
How can we remember that Jesus
is always with us—in the Eucharist
and in each other?

Visit our
web site at
www.FaithFirst.com

The Church's Year

17

We Pray

Father,
it is our duty
and our salvation,
always and
everywhere to give
you thanks through
your beloved Son,
Jesus Christ.

*Preface, Eucharistic
Prayer II*

Winter, spring,
summer, and fall are
the seasons of the
year. The Church's
year has seasons too.
What are the names
of those seasons?

*During the Easter
season we may see the
butterfly used as a
symbol for the Risen
Christ.*

171

Faith Focus

What is the liturgical year?

Faith Vocabulary

liturgy
The liturgy is the Church's work of worshiping God.

liturgical year
The seasons and feasts that make up the Church's year of worship is known as the liturgical year.

Celebrating is always fun. Throughout the year you and your family remember and celebrate many important occasions. You celebrate birthdays and anniversaries. You celebrate other days on which something wonderful happened.

Our Church's Year of Worship

Our church community also gathers to celebrate. We gather especially to celebrate the work of Jesus our Savior and to worship God at the **liturgy.** Liturgy is the name we give to the Church's worship. The word *liturgy* means "the work of the people." At the liturgy the church community praises and thanks God the Father for creation and for the gift of God's Son, Jesus Christ, our Savior.

All through the year the church community gathers to worship God. The Church's year of prayer and worship is called the **liturgical year.** It is made up of seasons and feasts that celebrate and remember God's great love for us.

The liturgical year begins on the First Sunday of Advent. During Advent we prepare for Christmas.

The Christmas season begins on Christmas Eve. During the Christmas season we praise and thank God for sending us Jesus, the Savior of the world.

The days of Lent prepare us for Easter. During the Easter season we celebrate and remember Jesus' Resurrection.

During Ordinary Time we recall the life, teachings, and mission of Jesus. We learn how to live as followers of Jesus.

To Help You Remember

1. What do we call the Church's year of seasons and feasts?

2. How do you celebrate the seasons of the Church's year with your parish?

Picturing the Liturgical Year

Each picture reminds us of one of the seasons of the Church's year. Write the name of the season beside the correct number.

1. _____

2. _____

3. _____

4. _____

Faith Focus

When does the church community celebrate the Paschal mystery most fully?

Faith Vocabulary

Easter Triduum
The Easter Triduum includes Holy Thursday, Good Friday, and the celebrations of the Easter Vigil and Easter Sunday.

With My Family

Find out what liturgical season it is now. Make placemats for your dinner table that help your family celebrate and remember the liturgical season. Be creative!

Celebrating the Paschal Mystery

Just as our family and our country have important times of the year, so does our church community. Lent and Easter are the liturgical seasons that prepare us for and help us to celebrate the Paschal mystery in its fullness. The Paschal mystery is the celebration of Jesus' suffering, dying, and being raised to new life.

The center of the liturgical year is the **Easter Triduum.** The Triduum includes Holy Thursday, Good Friday, and the celebrations of the Easter Vigil and Easter Sunday. During these three days we remember that Jesus died and was raised to new life for us.

To Help You Remember

1. What do we celebrate during the seasons of Lent and Easter?

2. Why are these two seasons important?

The Events of the Easter Triduum

Draw a picture, write a poem, or tell a story about the Easter Triduum.

Faith Vocabulary

Ordinary Time
Ordinary Time includes the weeks of the liturgical year that are not the seasons of Advent, Christmas, Lent, or Easter.

The Church Celebrates Ordinary Time

Ordinary Time is our Church's longest season of the year. Ordinary Time takes place twice during the liturgical year. The first part of Ordinary Time begins after the Christmas season and continues until Lent. The second part of Ordinary Time takes place after the Easter season and continues until Advent.

The Widow's Offering.
Mark 12:41–44

The Sower and the Seed.
Mark 4:2–9

The Raising of Lazarus.
John 11:1–45

During Ordinary Time we listen to stories from the Gospel that tell us about Jesus' life, his teachings, and his work while he was on earth. Sometimes we might listen to one of Jesus' parables. This kind of story teaches a lesson about how much God loves us, what the kingdom of God is like, or how we are to act as Jesus' followers.

Other times we might listen to a story about one of the miracles Jesus worked. Through these miracles Jesus healed people, raised people from the dead, and did many other amazing things.

By listening to all the gospel stories, we come to know Jesus more and more. We listen to Jesus and learn how we can live as his followers.

To Help You Remember

1. What is Ordinary Time?

2. Why is Ordinary Time important?

Your Favorite Gospel Stories

Complete the sentences about your favorite gospel story.

One of my favorite gospel stories is

_____.

This story teaches me

_____
_____
_____
_____.

During the liturgical year our church family remembers and celebrates the many important events in the life of Jesus. We use special colors to remind us of each season of the Church's year.

Liturgical Colors

Read about the colors the Church uses throughout the liturgical year. These colors help us to celebrate each season.

What season is the Church celebrating right now? Look for the liturgical colors being used in your church this Sunday.

ADVENT
(Purple or violet)
Reminds us to prepare for Jesus' coming.

Christmas
(White or Gold)
Reminds us to be joyful about the coming of Jesus.

Ordinary Time
(Green)
Reminds us to be faithful to the teachings of Jesus.

LENT (Purple or violet)
Reminds us to be sorry for our sins and to try to live better lives.

Holy Thursday (White or Gold)
Reminds us to be thankful for Jesus' gift of the Eucharist.

Good Friday
(Red)
Reminds us to remember Jesus' dying on the cross.

Easter
(White or Gold)
Reminds us to rejoice. Jesus is alive!

The Church's liturgical year helps you to keep your faith alive. It gives you an opportunity to learn more about the Holy Trinity and to move from one season of faith into another.

Helping Me to Remember Jesus

Think about the liturgical season the Church is celebrating now. What do you like about it? What does it help you to remember about Jesus?

_____

_____

_____

_____

_____

_____

My Faith Choice

This week I am going to remember this event in the life of Jesus: _____ .
I can do this by

_____ .

And now we pray.

We thank you, God, for everything you have done for us.
Based on Psalm 15:2

Use the clues to complete this crossword puzzle.

DOWN

1. The Church's work of worshiping God
2. The season that celebrates Jesus, the Son of God, coming to us as our Savior
3. The time of the Church's year when we remember Jesus' being raised from the dead

5. The time of the Church's year when we prepare for Christmas

ACROSS

4. The suffering, death, and Resurrection of Jesus
6. The time of the Church's year when we get ready for Easter

Answer the following questions.

1. What are the seasons of the liturgical year?

_____

2. Why does the Church celebrate the liturgical year?

_____

3. How do you celebrate the seasons of the liturgical year?

_____

Think and share with your family.

How can our family better understand and celebrate the seasons and feasts of the liturgical year?

Visit our web site at www.FaithFirst.com

Parent Page—Unit 3: We Live

Your Role

One day a man took his twelve-year-old son to the movies. He asked for two adult tickets. The ticket agent commented that the man's son was small for his age, and could easily have passed for eleven. "If you could have fooled me and gotten him in for a child's price," the ticket agent asked, "why didn't you? Who would have known the difference?" The man replied, "My son would have known." As parents we have the awesome responsibility of being the examples that our children see of what it means to be a Christian. Your child's idea of right and wrong is greatly influenced by what you do, the actions you take, and the decisions that you make. It is very helpful at this stage of your child's development to talk with your child about the decisions that you make and how you choose not only between right and wrong but also between good and better.

What We're Teaching

The focus of this unit is morality. The unit begins with the law of love and gives your child some practical examples of what this means in today's world. We review the Ten Commandments and help your child to understand how keeping each commandment helps them to love God, themselves, and others. We also teach about God's gift of grace and our belief in life everlasting. We discuss the meaning of stewardship and the importance of each choice we make.

Visit our web site at www.FaithFirst.com

What Difference Does It Make?

How we live—how we act and how we treat others—is the way in which we show the world who we are and what we believe. And it is how we act with those closest to us, with our family, that makes all the difference. We choose our values and then we live by them. Sometimes it doesn't seem that we have made a conscious choice, but even not choosing is making a choice. It is good from time to time to review how we are living. Are we doing for others? Are we sharing our time and talents as well as our financial resources with those less fortunate than we are? What percentage of our time do we spend thinking about others? It is good to remind ourselves that God cares little about how much money we make or how many things we acquire. It is what we do with these things that matters.

Unit Opener Photographs: (top left) stained-glass window depicting the Ten Commandments; (top right) living God's call to love one another; (bottom) the beauty and goodness of God's creation.

Jesus Teaches Us How to Love

A Scripture Story

18

We Pray

Almighty and ever-living God, may we do with loving hearts what you ask of us and come to share the life you promise.

Based on Opening Prayer 30th Sunday in Ordinary Time

Jesus teaches us to love God above all else. Jesus also teaches us to love ourselves and others. What does this mean in your life?

"You shall love your neighbor as yourself."
Matthew 22:40

How many times a day do you hear someone say, "I promise"? Making and keeping promises is something we do all the time.

God's Special Promise

In the very beginning of the Bible we read about a promise. We learn that our first parents made a promise to God. They promised to obey God.

The Bible also tells us that our first parents broke their promise to God. We call this broken promise original sin. Because our first parents sinned they broke their friendship with God. They lost the happiness God first gave them.

What did God do? He made a promise to them. He would send them someone who would help people live as true friends of God. He would show them how to keep their promises to God.

God's promise to people is called the **covenant.** The covenant is the solemn promise between God and his people.

Faith Focus

What was the promise God made with his people?

Faith Vocabulary

covenant
The covenant is the solemn agreement between God and the Israelites.

The story of Noah and the great flood is about the covenant God made with all people. The rainbow in the sky is a sign that God will always keep his promises. The covenant will last forever.

The Bible story of Abraham is also about God's covenant with his people. God promised Abraham that he would be the father of God's people.

Many years later God made a covenant with Moses. God gave Moses the Ten Commandments. The Commandments tell us how to live our covenant with God. They show us how to keep our promises to God and to one another. They show us how to love God and one another. Living the Ten Commandments guides us to find true happiness now and with God forever in heaven.

To Help You Remember

1. What was the promise God made with his people called?

2. Who are some of the leaders who helped God's people keep the covenant?

One Promise

If you could make just one promise that will help you be a good friend, what would it be? Write your promise in the banner and decorate the banner.

Reading the Word of God

Faith Focus

What does Jesus teach us about the Great Commandment?

Faith Vocabulary

Great Commandment
The Great Commandment is the commandment that all of God's laws depend on. It is, "You shall love God with all your heart, soul, and mind. You shall love others as you love yourself."

With My Family

Make up a list of rules that will help your family live as children of God. Talk about each rule and how it will help you to be fair and loving. Post the list on the refrigerator door and read it often.

God kept his promise to send someone who would help people live as true friends of God. God sent us his Son, Jesus. Jesus showed us how to keep our promises to God. Jesus taught us to live the **Great Commandment.**

Jesus Teaches Us

Jesus was one of the greatest teachers who ever lived. He taught large crowds of people. He also taught individuals. He even taught religious leaders more about God.

One day Jesus taught a very special lesson about God's law. A teacher of the law asked Jesus, "Which commandment in the law is the greatest?" Jesus then taught the man the Great Commandment.

Jesus said, " 'Love God with all your heart, soul, and mind.' This is the greatest and the first commandment."

Then Jesus said, "The second commandment is like it: 'You shall love your neighbor as yourself.' The whole law depends on these two commandments."

Based on Matthew 22:34–38

To Help You Remember

1. What are the two parts of the Great Commandment?

2. Why is it important to live the Great Commandment?

Living the Great Commandment

Draw a red heart beside the ways you can show your love for God.

Draw a blue heart beside the ways you can show your love for others.

Draw a green heart beside the ways you can show love for yourself.

(Hint: You may draw more than one heart for some statements!)

I will say my prayers each day.

I will go to bed on time.

I will always wear my seat belt.

I will play fairly at recess.

I will go to Mass each week.

I will share with others.

Understanding the Word of God

Love for Ourselves

Jesus' words tell us that the Great Commandment has two parts. It is not enough to show love to God through prayer and worship. We also need to love our neighbor as ourselves.

We show our love for God by the way we treat ourselves. We develop and use the gifts and talents God gave us. We treat our bodies with care. We know that we are created in God's image. We love and respect ourselves.

Love for Others

We also show our love for God by the way we treat others. We respect and care for all people. We treat people with kindness. We respect their bodies and their feelings. We know that all people are created in God's image.

Jesus taught us that loving others also includes loving our enemies. This is not an easy thing to do. But it is part of Jesus' commandment of love.

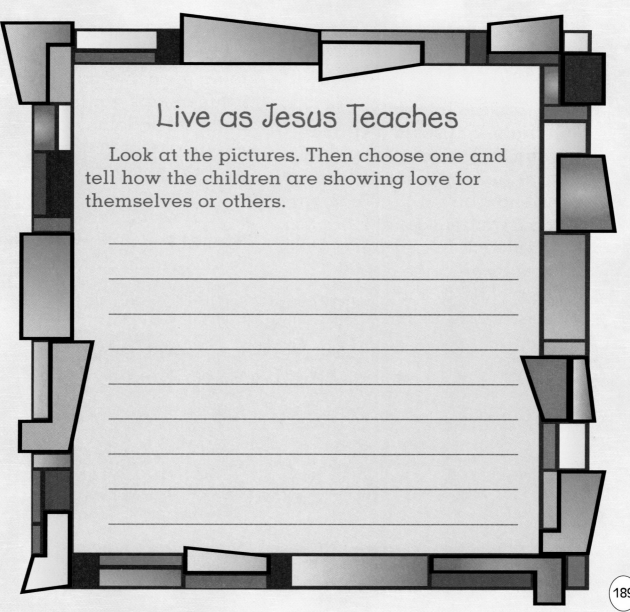

Live as Jesus Teaches

Look at the pictures. Then choose one and tell how the children are showing love for themselves or others.

_____

_____

_____

_____

_____

_____

_____

_____

Jesus taught us that all the commandments depend on the Great Commandment. When we live according to the Great Commandment, we are doing what Jesus taught us.

Be a Teacher for Good

There have been many great teachers in the history of our Church. They have taught us how to live lives of doing good for others.

You are a teacher too. That might seem a strange way to describe you, but it is true. When you help a friend, you teach. When you do a random act of kindness, you teach. When you are the first to welcome a new child to your school, you teach.

You teach others by how you act. You teach by showing others acts of virtue. Virtue simply means doing good. Living a life of virtue means getting into the habit of doing good for others and for yourself. It is what love is all about.

Name someone who teaches you how to live the Great Commandment.

It feels good to do good. Not only do you feel good, but others do too. It is easy to spot people who do good. They smile a lot. And they make other people smile too.

Doing Something Good

Draw yourself doing something good for someone else. Then sign your first name.

My Faith Choice

During the coming week I will try to do what I pictured in the activity.

And now we pray.

Teach me your ways, O LORD. I will carefully follow them.
Based on Psalm 119:33

Match the words in column A with
their definitions in column B.

_____ 1. rainbow

_____ 2. covenant

_____ 3. Moses

_____ 4. Abraham

a. father of God's people

b. the person to whom God gave the Ten Commandments

c. a sign that God's covenant will last forever

d. God's promise to enter into a solemn agreement with the Israelites

Fill in the blanks to complete the words
of the Great Commandment.

Jesus said, "Love God with all your _____ ,

soul, and mind. Love your _____

as you love _____ ."

Based on Matthew 22:37–39

Think and share with your family.
How can our family better live
the Great Commandment?

Visit our
web site at
www.FaithFirst.com

The Commandments Teach Us to Love

We Pray

Blessed be Jesus,
whom you sent
to be our friend.
He came to show us
how to love you,
Father,
by loving one
another.

*Based on Eucharistic
Prayer for Masses with
Children, II*

We are learning to live as children of God. The Ten Commandments help us to love God, others, and ourselves. What are some of the Ten Commandments you already know?

The Commandments help us to live as God's children.

Living the Commandments

Faith Vocabulary

Ten Commandments
The Ten Commandments are the laws given by God to Moses on Mount Sinai. The Ten Commandments help us to love God, others, and ourselves.

Everywhere we go, there are rules and laws we must obey. We follow rules at school, at home, and in our community. Why are rules and laws important?

God's Laws

The **Ten Commandments** are laws given to us by God. They tell us how to love God, others, and ourselves.

God gave the Ten Commandments to Moses. Moses was one of the first great leaders of God's people, the Israelites. Here is the story of Moses and the Ten Commandments.

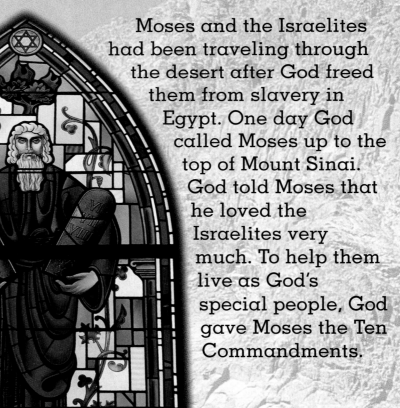

Stained-glass window of Moses holding the Commandments on background of Mount Sinai.

Moses and the Israelites had been traveling through the desert after God freed them from slavery in Egypt. One day God called Moses up to the top of Mount Sinai. God told Moses that he loved the Israelites very much. To help them live as God's special people, God gave Moses the Ten Commandments.

I am the LORD your God: you shall not
    have any other gods before me.
You shall not take the name of the
    LORD your God in vain.
Remember to keep holy the LORD's Day.
Honor your father and your mother.
You shall not kill.
You shall not commit adultery.
You shall not steal.
You shall not bear false witness
    against your neighbor.
You shall not covet your neighbor's wife.
You shall not covet your neighbor's
    goods.

                    Based on Exodus 20:1–17

To Help You Remember

1. To whom did God give the Ten Commandments?

2. Why did God give us the Ten Commandments?

Moses took the laws that God had given him and went down from the mountain. He explained the laws to the Israelites, who agreed to obey them.

The Ten Commandments helped the Israelites to live as God's special people. They help us to live as God's special people too.

Living the Commandments

Write one way the Ten Commandments help us to live as Jesus' followers at home and in school.

While we might think of a law as a rule that won't let us do something, we may not think about how it really helps us.

Showing Our Love for God

The Ten Commandments are the same way. When we look at them one way, we think that they are telling us only about things we should not do. But if we look at them in another way, we can see how they help us to do things that show our love and respect for God and others. This really helps us! The first three commandments help us to show our love and respect for God.

1. I am the LORD your God. You shall not have other gods before me.

This means that we know God is more important than anything else.

2. You shall not take the name of the LORD your God in vain.

This means that we respect the name of God. Our names are important and God's name is as well.

3. Remember to keep holy the LORD's Day.

This means that we must take part in the celebration of Mass on Sunday. It also means that we should treat Sunday as a special day.

To Help You Remember

1. What do the Ten Commandments help us to do?

2. What do the first three commandments teach us?

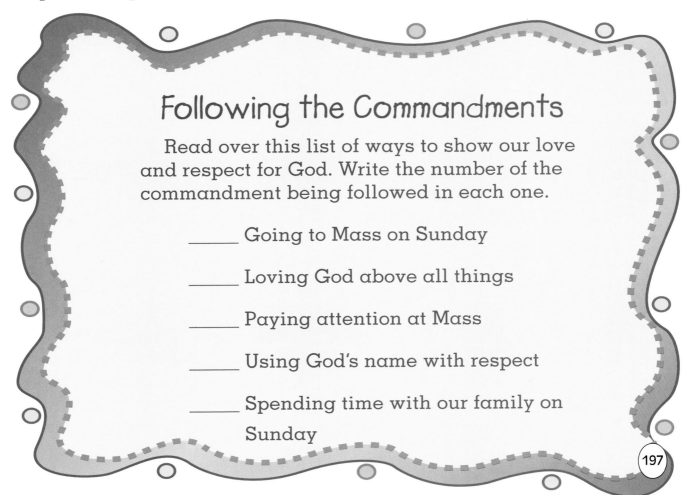

Following the Commandments

Read over this list of ways to show our love and respect for God. Write the number of the commandment being followed in each one.

_____ Going to Mass on Sunday

_____ Loving God above all things

_____ Paying attention at Mass

_____ Using God's name with respect

_____ Spending time with our family on Sunday

The Love of the Trinity

The first three commandments tell us how we should love God. They give us ways that we can respect his name and keep his day holy. Everything we are and everything we have comes from God. God loves us even more than we love ourselves!

God is love, and God teaches us how we should love not only him but each other. You have learned about the Holy Trinity. You know that there is only one God in three Persons—the Father, the Son, and the Holy Spirit.

These three Persons in God love each other with a perfect love. That is something that is very hard for us to imagine. Even though we love our parents and friends very much, we still get angry with them and sometimes they disappoint us. But this never happens in the Trinity.

God Is Love

The special love that the three Persons in the Trinity have for each other is not like any love that we see on earth. From the Holy Trinity we learn to love others. The Father loves Jesus and Jesus loves the Father and the Holy Spirit. They are the model for us of how to love.

This is sometimes very hard for us to understand. But we can remember it. And each time we think about being mean to someone or hurting someone, we can try to act more like God and Jesus and the Holy Spirit.

How to Love

Unscramble the letters to discover how we are to love others. Let the capital letters help you.

evoL yltcefrep sa ruoy rehtaF sevol yltcefrep.

_____ _____ ____

_____ _____ _____

_____ .

The first three commandments help us to show our love for God. The Trinity is a model of the love we are to have for one another. One important way that we show our love for God is by gathering for Eucharist every Sunday. But there are other days when we need to show our love for God and take part in the celebration of Mass also.

Holy Days of Obligation

During the church year there are six days in the United States that the Church asks us to take part in the celebration of Mass. The days celebrate important times in the life of Jesus, Mary, and the saints. These six days are called holy days of obligation. On these days we are called together as God's people to celebrate the Eucharist.

The six holy days of obligation in the United States are the Solemnity of Mary, the Ascension of Our Lord, the Assumption of the Blessed Virgin Mary, All Saints' Day, Mary's Immaculate Conception, and Christmas.

Why do you think we should take part in the celebration of Mass on these days?

Solemnity of Mary

Ascension of Our Lord

Assumption of the Blessed Virgin Mary

All Saints' Day

Mary's Immaculate Conception

Christmas

Sunday is an important day for you, your family, and your parish family. You and your family join other families in your parish for the celebration of Mass. Together you show your love for God and for one another.

God's Special Day

Think about some of the special days you and your family celebrate.

How do you feel when people celebrate a special day with you?

_____

Why is it important to celebrate special days in our life with people we love?

_____

Why is it important for our church family to celebrate Sundays together?

_____

My Faith Choice

Something that I can do this Sunday (and every Sunday) to show God and others that I honor his special day is

_____ .

And now we pray.

Happy the child of God who finds happiness in the law of the LORD and thinks about God's law day and night.
Based on Psalm 1:1–2

Complete the story of Moses and the Ten Commandments.

Moses was one of the first leaders of the

(1) _____ . God brought

Moses to the top of (2) _____ .

God told Moses that he loved the Israelites

very much and wanted them to be his

(3) _____ . God then gave

Moses a set of laws, which we call the

(4) _____ .

The laws God gave to Moses show us how

to love (5) _____ .

Answer the questions by writing your responses on the lines provided.

1. What do the Ten Commandments help us to do?

   _____

   _____

2. Why did God give us the Ten Commandments?

   _____

   _____

3. Who is our example of perfect love? _____

Think and share with your family.

Jesus asks us to love one another as he loves us. What are some ways we can do that?

Visit our
web site at
www.FaithFirst.com

We Love and Respect One Another

We Pray

Father,
help us to live
as the holy family,
united in respect
and love.
Amen.

*Taken from the
Opening Prayer for the
Feast of the Holy Family*

We know that God created us in his image. God loves us and asks us to love and respect one another. In what ways do we show our respect for one another?

"Love one another as I love you."

John 15:12

203

Wouldn't it be great if people always treated you fairly? If they always listened to your side of the story? If they thought the best of you? What if everyone was always kind to you and always tried to help you in any way they could? Living in a world like that would make you feel very good about yourself and about others as well.

Faith Focus

How does God want us to show our love for one another?

Faith Vocabulary

respect
Respect means "to look up to," "to honor," or "to admire."

A World of Love

That is the kind of world we might have if everyone did what God calls us to do. In the first letter John wrote to the early Christians, he said,

Beloved, if God so loved us, we also must love one another.
Based on 1 John 4:11

When John speaks about love, he is talking about the kind of love that helps us to treat others the way God wants us to.

God gave us very clear instructions on how we are to treat one another. The last seven of the Ten Commandments help us to treat others and ourselves with **respect** and care. They show us how to love God, ourselves, and others.

An Important Message

Use the code to discover another message that John wrote.

To Help You Remember

1. What do the last seven of the Ten Commandments tell us to do?

2. How can we show our love and respect for one another?

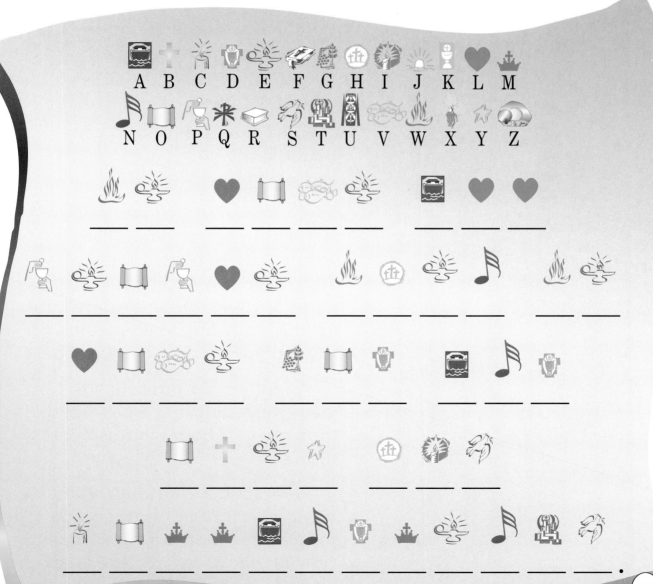

Showing Love for Others

Each of the last seven commandments teaches us something about our relationship with others. Let's look at them one at a time.

4. Honor your father and your mother.

We live the Fourth Commandment by loving and respecting our parents. That is easy to say but sometimes difficult to do. We honor our parents when we listen carefully to what they say to us instead of thinking of ways to answer back.

We honor our parents when we realize that they know more than we do about what is good for us.

We honor our parents when we appreciate all that they do for us and when we show them how much we appreciate what they do.

We honor them when we care for our clothes, our books, our food, our homes, and all the things that they provide for us.

The Church tells us that our family is like a church. Your family is a small community of the People of God who are part of the larger community of God. That is why the Church calls your family a domestic church. The word *domestic* means "home." Being a good Christian begins with our families, our domestic church.

To Help You Remember

1. What does the Fourth Commandment teach us?

2. How do we live out the Fourth Commandment?

With My Family

The next time you are together with your family, talk about the ways you show you care for each other.

My Family

List two ways in which your family is like the larger church community.

1. _____

_____

2. _____

_____

Faith Focus

What do the Fifth through Tenth Commandments tell us about living as children of God?

Faith Vocabulary

covet
Covet means "to want what someone else has."

5. You shall not kill.

God meant for all of us to enjoy the gift of life that he has given us. Life is sacred. It is not our right to take life away from anyone else.

The Fifth Commandment commands us to take great care of the life that we have been given. We keep this commandment when we treat our bodies with care. We also live this commandment when we avoid situations that we know are dangerous and when we help others to do the same.

6. You shall not commit adultery.

Married people live this commandment when they are faithful in their friendship with one another. We can prepare to live this commandment when we are faithful to our family and friends now.

7. You shall not steal.

We live this commandment when we respect what belongs to other people. We do not take anything from a store without paying for it. We do not cheat on tests. We are careful when we borrow and use the things that belong to other people.

To Help You Remember

1. What do the Fifth through Tenth Commandments teach us?

2. How do we show our love and respect for one another?

8. You shall not bear false witness against your neighbor.

We live this commandment when we are careful to say only the truth about other people. We do not tell lies. We do not say things that will hurt others.

9. You shall not covet your neighbor's wife.

10. You shall not covet your neighbor's goods.

The Ninth and Tenth Commandments both have to do with coveting. To **covet** means to want something that belongs to someone else that we do not have a right to make our own. We live these commandments when we are not jealous or greedy.

What They Mean to Me

Choose four of the commandments and rewrite them in your own words.

1. _____
_____

2. _____
_____

3. _____
_____

4. _____
_____

209

The First Letter of John reminds us that if we really love God, we must also love others. The most important reason that we treat others with love is because of who we are!

We Are Images of God

We are images of God. What does that mean? It means that when people look at us and at the way we act, they should see God reflected in us.

In our church communities that means that all of us should work very hard at getting along. Our churches should be places where people feel welcomed to stop and pray or meet and belong. They are places where we collect food for those who are hungry and clothes for those who need them.

In our churches we should see the love of God put into action by the people who are part of our parish community.

How is your parish church an image of God?

Each day you try in many ways to live the Ten Commandments. You pray. You are kind and generous. You are trustworthy and honest.

Keeping the Ten Commandments

Choose one of the Ten Commandments. In the box draw a sign or a symbol for that commandment. Explain how living that commandment can make your community a better place.

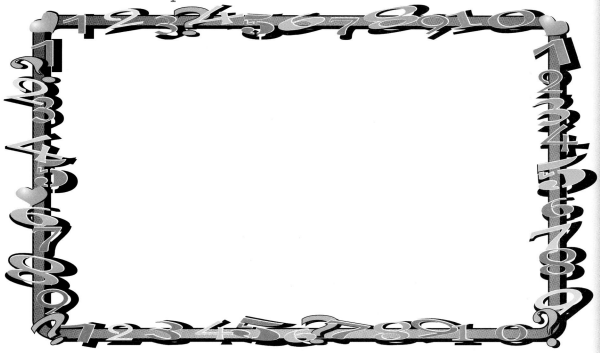

My Faith Choice

Write down one thing that you can do each day this week to follow God's laws better. I will try to

_____ .

And now we pray.

LORD, help me keep your law with all my heart.
Based on Psalm 119:9–10

Cross out the four sentences that are not one of the Ten Commandments.

1. Honor your father and your mother.
2. You shall not kill.
3. You shall not be angry.
4. You shall not commit adultery.
5. You shall not beg.
6. You shall not steal.
7. You shall bear false witness against your neighbor.
8. You shall not covet your neighbor's wife.
9. You shall not swear.
10. You shall not covet your neighbor's goods.

Answer the following questions

1. What do the last seven of the Ten Commandments tell us about how to treat others? _____
_____

2. What does the Fourth Commandment ask us to do?
_____
_____

3. How can we obey the Eighth Commandment?

_____
_____

Think and share with your family.
What will we do to show love and respect for each member of our family this week?

Visit our
web site at
www.FaithFirst.com

The Psalms and Stewardship

A Scripture Story

We Pray

O God, the earth has
given us its
harvest.
You have blessed us.
Based on Psalm 67:7

People of faith thank God for creation in many different ways. Sometimes they pray psalms to thank God for the beauty and goodness of creation. What are psalms?

*I will sing to the LORD
all my life;
I will sing praise
to my God.*
Based on Psalm 104:33

Most of us enjoy music. If you could write a song, what melody would you compose? What words, or lyrics, would you write?

Sacred Songs

Long ago the Jewish people wrote some sacred, or holy, songs called psalms. They used these songs to pray. These psalms are found in the Old Testament.

King **David** wrote many of the psalms. He was an ancestor of Jesus. The king loved God so much that he sang songs to God. In these songs he praised and thanked God. He also expressed sorrow for his sins.

Psalms as Prayers

The psalms are important prayers. Jesus learned them when he was a young boy. Then he prayed them all his life.

We too pray the psalms today. Some psalms praise God and tell him about our needs. We call these laments. We pray other psalms to learn wisdom. These wisdom psalms give practical advice about how we can live as God's children.

We also pray psalms to thank God for the gifts of creation. These thanksgiving psalms help us to remember that we join with all creation to thank God for all his blessings.

Long ago the Jewish people collected their many psalms of praise, lament, thanksgiving, and wisdom into a book. We call this the Book of Psalms. It contains 150 prayer-songs to God.

To Help You Remember

1. What is a psalm?

2. Name four reasons why we pray the psalms.

Decode a Prayer of Thanksgiving

The psalms are sacred prayer-songs. Use the code to discover one verse from a psalm of thanksgiving.

A	B	C	D	E	F	G	H	I	J	K	L	M
1	2	3	4	5	6	7	8	9	10	11	12	13

N	O	P	Q	R	S	T	U	V	W	X	Y	Z
14	15	16	17	18	19	20	21	22	23	24	25	26

O   G   O   D,   T   H   E
15   7   15 4   20 8   5

E   A   R   T   H   H   A   S
5   1   18   20 8   8   1   19

G   I   E   N   U   S
7   9   22 5   14   21 19

___ ___ ___   ___ ___ ___ ___ ___ ___ ___ .
9   20   19   8   1   18   22   5   19   20

Based on Psalm 67:7

Reading the Word of God

Here is a psalm that people have sung to God for many, many years. In this psalm we praise and thank God for creation. It reminds us that God cares for all creation.

Faith Focus

How does Psalm 104 help us to remember the beauty of God's world?

Psalm 104

O God, you are great!
You spread out the heavens like a tent!
You ride on the clouds!
Wind is your messenger.
Fire works for you.

You fixed the earth in the universe.
You made the ocean cover it like a coat.
You fixed the mountains in place.

You make small streams become
   mighty rivers.
They flow through the tall mountains.
They give drink to all animals.
Birds rest and sing beside your waters.

You make the moon to mark the
    passing of the seasons.
You make the sun to know the hour
    of its setting.
You bring darkness, and night falls.
Then young lions roam the earth.
You make the sun rise.
Then the lions go to their dens.
People go to work.

What wonderful work you have done,
    O God!

Based on Psalm 104

To Help You Remember

1. What are some things God has created?

2. How does God show his care for all creation?

With My Family

Share the psalm you wrote in the activity with your family. Pray the psalm together. Each week add another thing in creation you want to thank God for.

Thanking God for Creation

Add a word to each line to complete this prayer of thanksgiving.

O God, you are great and wonderful! I thank you

for **puppies** and **p**_____ ,

for **rain** and **r** _____ ,

for **antelope** and **a** _____ ,

for **iguanas** and **i** _____ ,

for **seals** and **s** _____ ,

for **elephants** and **e** _____ . Amen.

Understanding the Word of God

Faith Focus

How can praying Psalm 104 help us to live the Seventh Commandment?

Faith Vocabulary

stewards
People who have the responsibility to care for the things they have been given are called stewards.

What are you most thankful for in God's creation? Think of one way you help God keep creation beautiful.

We Care for God's World

Psalm 104 reminds us that God gave us the great gifts of nature. We see God's beauty in rocky mountains and soft rain. We hear God's goodness in birds' songs and in children's laughter.

God asks us to take care of all this beauty and goodness. One of our responsibilities as human beings is to take care of all that God created.

Living the Seventh Commandment

The Seventh Commandment is "You shall not steal." One of the ways to live the Seventh Commandment is to take care of creation. When we destroy it, we steal its beauty from others.

God wants us to take care of the world and all living creatures. When we do that, we become good **stewards** of creation.

We take care of creation so that all people can enjoy it. We refuse to be selfish and greedy and use up the gifts of creation. We share God's beauty and goodness with everyone.

As good stewards we can pray Psalm 104 and say to God,

May your glory last forever.
I will sing to you all my life.
I will be happy because of your
    goodness.
Alleluia!

Based on Psalm 104:31–35

Our job as stewards is to care for God's beauty and goodness and glory in our world. When we do this, we are living the Seventh Commandment.

To Help You Remember

1. What is a steward of creation?

2. What can stewards do to take care of God's creation?

Living as Good Stewards

Write a letter to a friend telling them what it means to be a steward of God's creation.

_____

_____

_____

_____

_____

_____

_____

For many, many years people have used psalms to pray. We praise God with psalms. We say we are sorry. We thank God for creation.

Thanking God for the Harvest

As stewards of God's creation, we thank God for all that is good and beautiful in our world. In farm communities, people sometimes go to church to celebrate the harvest. Harvest is the time when they bring the ripe crops into their barns.

God gave the farmers the fruits of the trees. God gave them the golden grain of the fields. God sent them the gentle rain and the warm sunrays. For all this goodness, the farmers thank God.

At the Mass after the Harvest, the farmers pray a psalm of thanksgiving. They thank God for helping them to be good stewards. The psalm they pray is Psalm 67. The words they keep repeating are

O God, the earth has given us its harvest.
You have blessed us.

Based on Psalm 67:7

The Church rejoices that the farmers have been good stewards of God's world.

When could you say this harvest psalm?

What Difference Does It Make in My Life?

God asks you to be a steward of creation. Psalm 104 reminds you of God's beauty and goodness in creation. When you pray this psalm, it helps you to remember to care for all that God has created.

Remembering God's Creation

Look at Psalm 104 on pages 216–217. Write your favorite part of the psalm. Pray it whenever you find yourself forgetting to care for God's creation.

My favorite lines from Psalm 104 are

____

____

____

____

____.

My Faith Choice

This week I will be a good steward of creation by

__________________________.

And now we pray.

What wonderful work you have done, O God!

Based on Psalm 104:24

Complete the sentences with a word from the word bank.

| David | psalms | stewards |

1. We call the sacred songs or poems found in the Old Testament _____.

2. One person who wrote some of the psalms is King _____.

3. When we pray Psalm 104, we remember to take care of God's creation. Then we are being good _____.

Answer the following questions.

1. How does a good steward take care of God's creation?

_____

_____

_____

2. Why is taking care of God's creation important?

_____

_____

_____

Think and share with your family.

Talk with your family about the beauty of God's creation. Then pray Psalm 104 together.

Visit our
web site at
www.FaithFirst.com

God Shares His Life with Us

22

We Pray

Eternal rest
grant unto them,
O Lord.
And let perpetual
light shine upon them.
May they rest
in peace.
Amen.

*From the Order of
Christian Funerals*

God shares his life
with us. God offers
us the gift of eternal
life, or heaven. When
you hear the word
heaven, what do
you think of?

The LORD is my light.
Psalm 27:1

223

The Gift of Grace

Faith Focus

What is grace?

Faith Vocabulary

grace
The gift of our sharing in the life of the Holy Trinity is called grace.

sanctifying grace
Sanctifying grace is the grace we receive at Baptism. It makes us holy. It makes us like God.

actual grace
Actual grace is the grace given to us by the Holy Spirit to help us follow Jesus.

Every family member shares in the life of his or her family. How do you share in your family's life?

God Calls Us to Share in His Life

God created us to share in the life and love of the Holy Trinity. Sharing in the life of God the Father, Son, and Holy Spirit is a gift from God. We call this gift **grace.** The word *grace* means "gift" or "favor."

There are two kinds of grace, **sanctifying grace** and **actual grace.** The word *sanctify* means "to make holy or sacred." Sanctifying grace makes us children of God. We receive the gift of sanctifying grace at Baptism.

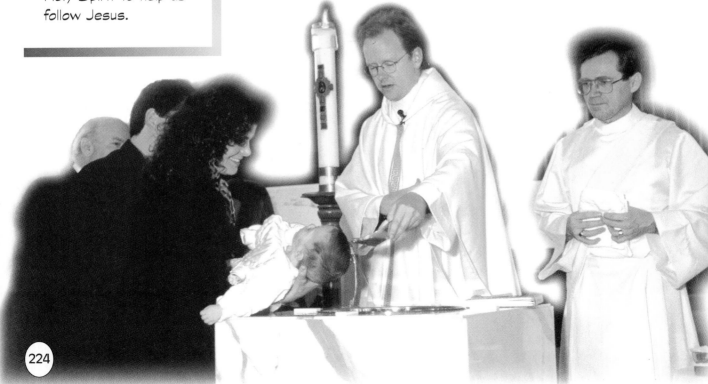

Actual grace comes to us through the Holy Spirit. The Holy Spirit helps us live as children of God. The Spirit helps us live as followers of Jesus.

Actual grace helps us to make good choices and to stay away from sinful choices. Actual grace helps us to live as Jesus taught us to live.

To Help You Remember

1. What does the word grace mean?

2. How does grace help us share in God's life?

Grace Helps Us to Live Like Jesus

For each description of how Jesus lived, name one way you could follow his example.

1. Jesus feeds five thousand people.

   I can _____

   _____ .

2. Jesus reaches out in kindness and blesses the children.

   I can _____

   _____ .

3. Jesus teaches us to help our neighbors.

   I can _____

   _____ .

Life is a wonderful gift from God. Right now you are alive on earth. When your body dies, God wants you to live with him forever.

God Calls Us to Eternal Life

You have learned that Jesus was raised from the dead. He lives with the Father and the Holy Spirit. We believe that God invites us to live with the Father, Jesus, and the Holy Spirit forever.

Jesus promised that all people who love God and live the commandments will live with God forever. We call this promise eternal life. The word *eternal* means "forever." We call our eternal life with God **heaven.**

Jesus made that promise to us at the Last Supper. Jesus promised that he would prepare a place for us in heaven. Read what Jesus promised.

Jesus said, "Do not let your hearts be troubled. Believe in God and believe in me. In my Father's house there are many rooms. I am going to prepare a place for you. I will come again. I will take you with me so that we can be together."

Based on John 14:1–3

We believe in Jesus' promise. We believe in life everlasting. When we pray the Nicene Creed at Mass, we say, "We look for the resurrection of the dead and the life of the world to come."

To Help You Remember

1. Who will live with God forever?

2. Why does God invite us to live with him forever?

With My Family

Spend some time this week with your family praying for those in your family who have died. Thank God for sharing eternal life with these loved ones.

My Images of Heaven

Draw a picture that shows what you think heaven might be like.

Faith Vocabulary

hell
    A life separated from God forever after death is called hell.

Some Choose to Turn Away

God invites all of us to live with him forever in heaven. Some people do not accept God's invitation. Instead, they choose to live their lives away from God. They separate themselves from God's love through sin.

Jesus told a parable about people who refuse God's invitation to live with him forever.

Jesus said, "A man sent his servants to invite his guests to a banquet. The people made the choice not to come.

"Again the man sent his servants to invite the guests. He told the servants to say, 'The feast is ready! My prize calf has been prepared.' Still the people made the choice not to come.

228

"The man became angry. He said to his servants, 'The invited guests do not deserve to come. Go into the streets and invite everyone you meet.'

"The servants went into the streets and invited people as the man told them to do. Soon the banquet hall was filled with guests."

Based on Luke 14:15–24

Jesus' story reminds us that God invites all of us to his eternal banquet, which we call heaven. By the way we live our lives, we can choose to accept God's gift of heaven or we can choose to separate ourselves from God forever. We call being separated from God forever **hell.** Those who choose to live without God in this life will live without God forever.

To Help You Remember

1. Who does God invite to live with him forever?

2. Why does God allow us to choose to live with him forever or be separated from him forever?

Growing in Your Love for God

Name something you can do each day to help you grow in your love for God.

_____

_____

_____

_____

_____

_____

Our church community believes that death is not the end of our life. We believe that God invites us to live with him forever in heaven.

We Believe in Life Everlasting

When a baptized Catholic dies, the church community gathers to celebrate the Mass of Christian Burial. Together we thank God for the gift of eternal life that has now been given to that person. The Church also prays that the person's family and friends may be strengthened in their belief that the person they love who has died is with God forever.

It is always sad when someone we love dies. Yet the followers of Jesus believe that life has not ended for the person who has died. Instead, life has only changed. Eternal life with God is God's great gift forever!

How does your parish community help those families who are sad because someone they love has died?

God shares his life and love with you. Every day of your life, God is always with you. God is always at your side.

God Is Always with Us

Each day the Holy Spirit helps you make good choices. In the circle draw or write about a good choice you made this week. On the lines write the names of people who were helped by your choice.

My Faith Choice

This week I will choose to accept God's gift of life and love by _____

_____ .

And now we pray.

Happy are those people whom you guide, LORD.
Based on Psalm 94:12

Chapter Review

Use the clues to complete this crossword puzzle.

DOWN
1. A life separated from God forever after death
2. The kind of grace that makes us holy
3. Eternal life with God

ACROSS
4. The gift of God's life and love to us
5. God's presence with us through the Holy Spirit, helping us to live as children of God

Answer the following questions.

1. What is grace?

_____

2. How does the Holy Spirit help us live as followers of Jesus?

_____

3. Why does God want us to live with him forever?

_____

Think and share with your family.

As a family, name some things you say or do every day that show that you want to live with God forever.

Visit our web site at www.FaithFirst.com

Parent Page—Unit 4: We Pray

Your Role

Your child learns what is important from you. If you keep in touch with family members, if you write thank-you notes, if you take the time and stop and say hello to neighbors, if you call your parents and grandparents, then your children learn how important it is to build and maintain relationships. This unit on prayer helps your child learn ways of staying in touch with God. Your child needs to see that you recognize the importance of communicating daily with God. Do you pray each day? Does your child know that you pray? Do you pray with your child? Sometimes prayer can be simple and informal; at other times you can use more formal, traditional prayers. What is important is that your child know and learn from your example how necessary prayer is to our life of faith.

What We're Teaching

The fourth unit focuses on the importance of prayer in our lives. The children learn that sometimes Jesus would sit and talk to God, the Father; sometimes he would just sit and listen to what God was saying to him. They will also learn about saints and about blessings. As a parent do you ever bless your child? At bedtime you might try tracing the sign of the cross on your child's forehead just as you did when he or she was baptized. This is a wonderful tradition to begin and continue in your family. The children will also learn about creeds, in particular the Apostles' Creed. The unit ends with a Scripture story of Mary and Elizabeth and the Hail Mary.

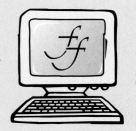

Visit our web site at
www.FaithFirst.com

What Difference Does It Make?

Communication in any relationship is vital. Without it, a relationship often stagnates or even ceases to be. It is that way with our relationship with God as well. Building a relationship takes time and energy, and in these days when both of those are so scarce, sometimes we can't even imagine how we will find time to pray. But without praying, our relationship with God diminishes. Think of old friends and neighbors that once were so close to you. Once we move away, and communication slows, our relationship with them slows down as well. If we are truly in touch with God, then our thoughts should turn to him many times throughout the day—to give thanks, to ask for something, just to pause and be one with him. Someone once said, "A day hemmed with prayer is unlikely to unravel." Sound advice. God does make a difference in our lives.

Unit Opener Photographs: (top left) statue of Jesus Christ, in whom we profess our faith; (top right) stained-glass window depicting Mary, the mother of God; (bottom) talking and listening to God in prayer.

God Invites Us to Pray

23

Our Father,
who art in heaven,
hallowed
be thy name.
From the Lord's Prayer

Jesus prayed and taught his disciples to pray. Who taught you how to pray? What are some of the ways you have learned to pray?

When we pray, we turn our minds and hearts to God.

When we care about someone, we like to talk with them. Even if they live far away, we can still talk with them on the phone, by E-mail, or in a letter. It is fun to get a phone call, an E-mail, or a letter from someone. We know that they are thinking about us and that they want to talk to us.

Jesus Prayed

When Jesus was on earth, he often thought about God his Father. Sometimes Jesus would sit and talk to God the Father; sometimes he would just sit and listen to what God was saying to him. This is prayer. We **pray** when we talk or listen to God.

Jesus prayed often. Many times he would pray alone. Sometimes he would pray with others.

On the night before he died, Jesus prayed with his disciples at the Last Supper. He asked God to keep them safe. After the meal they walked to a garden. He knew that he would soon be arrested and have to die.

While he was in the garden, he prayed. This shows us how much he trusted his Father. Jesus prayed that God would give him strength. Jesus said that he would do whatever God asked of him.

The next day the Roman soldiers nailed Jesus to a cross. He prayed, "Father, forgive them; they do not know what they are doing." Just before he died, Jesus said, "Father, I give myself to you."

Based on Luke 23:34, 46

To Help You Remember

1. What are some reasons Jesus prayed?

2. How did Jesus show his trust in God?

Throughout his whole life Jesus placed his trust in God the Father. He asked God to help him do the work the Father sent him to do. Jesus also asked his Father to help his disciples place their trust in the Father as he did.

My Prayer of Trust

Jesus trusted in God the Father completely. He asks us to place our trust in God the Father too. Complete these sentences to show how you can place trust in God.

Father, I trust you

_____.

Father, I trust you

_____.

Father, I trust you

_____.

Faith Vocabulary

Abba
Abba is a word that means "father" in the language Jesus spoke. Jesus used this word when he prayed to God the Father.

Lord's Prayer
The prayer that Jesus gave us is called the Lord's Prayer.

Our Father
Another name for the Lord's Prayer is the Our Father.

If someone asked you to teach them how to pray, what would you say?

Jesus Teaches Us How to Pray

You know that Jesus prayed often. Jesus' followers prayed too. But they wanted to learn to pray as Jesus prayed.

One day Jesus' disciples were with him when he was praying. When he was finished praying, they asked Jesus to teach them to pray.

Jesus said, "When you pray, say,
Father, holy be your name,
your kingdom come.
Give us each day our daily bread
and forgive us our sins
for we forgive anyone who has hurt us."
Based on Luke 11:1–4

When Jesus prayed, he called his Father in heaven **Abba.** Abba means "father" in the language Jesus spoke. Jesus teaches us that God is our Father too. We are all God's children.

Jesus told us to ask God our Father for our daily bread. This bread is more than food to keep our bodies alive. It is everything we need to live. When we ask God for daily bread, we ask for all that we and other people need to live as children of God.

We call the prayer Jesus gave us the **Lord's Prayer** or the **Our Father.** In this prayer we place our trust in God our Father.

To Help You Remember

1. Who asked Jesus to teach them to pray?

2. Why did Jesus call God Abba?

Abba, Father

Think about the prayer Jesus gave us. Then write a prayer to God the Father, using your own words.

_____

_____

_____

_____

_____

_____

_____

Faith Vocabulary

private prayer
   Private prayer is prayer a person prays alone.

public prayer
   Public prayer is prayer that people pray together.

Sometimes we want to be alone. When do you like to be alone? At other times we want to be with others. What are some of the things you do when you are with others?

Praying Alone and with Others

At times Jesus too wanted to be alone. When he was alone, the Gospel tells us that Jesus would pray to his Father. We call this kind of prayer **private prayer.**

We pray this way too. We enjoy being alone with God. We talk to and listen to God. We tell him about ourselves, our family, and our friends. We trust that God always listens to our prayers.

Jesus prayed in another way too. Jesus joined with his disciples to pray. He also prayed with others in the Temple in Jerusalem. Praying with others is called **public prayer.**

Catholics pray with others too. Our greatest public prayer is the Mass. We gather with one another to pray, to listen to readings from the Scriptures, and to celebrate and share in the Eucharist.

Ways to Pray

Draw a picture of yourself praying alone or with others in your favorite place to pray.

To Help You Remember

1. What is the difference between private prayer and public prayer?

2. How did Jesus pray?

With My Family

Talk with your family about those times when you pray in private and when you pray in public.

241

By his words and actions Jesus taught us to pray. Like Jesus we sometimes spend time alone with God in prayer. At other times, we join with others to pray. Praying is so important for us that we even call ourselves people of prayer.

Our Church Helps Us to Pray

The Catholic Church helps us to pray in many ways. At the front of the church there is usually a cross or a crucifix. The cross reminds us that Jesus died for us. People often kneel by the cross and pray to thank Jesus for giving his life for us.

There is also a lighted candle near the tabernacle in our church. The candle reminds us of Jesus' presence with us in the Eucharist. Catholics sometimes spend time alone in prayer in the presence of the Eucharist.

Sometimes there are statues of saints in our churches. People often pray to the saints to help them live better lives.

All around us are reminders of the importance of prayer.

Who do you know who prays often?

Every time you pray you show you trust in God. Your prayer shows you know that God loves you and cares about you.

When, Where, and How

You already know how to pray. Put a check mark next to those ways you pray now. Put a star next to those ways you would like to try.

____ 1. In my bedroom

____ 2. At my parish church

____ 3. With my family

____ 4. With my friends

____ 5. At school

____ 6. Kneeling down

____ 7. Aloud with another person

____ 8. With my arms extended

____ 9. With my eyes closed

____ 10. Outdoors

My Faith Choice

This week I will talk with _____ about how he or she prays. This week I will pray this prayer.

_____

_____

_____ .

And now we pray.

"Ask and it will be given to you. Seek and you will find. Knock and the door will be opened to you."
Based on Matthew 7:7

Match the words in column A with their definitions in column B.

Column A

_____ 1. prayer

_____ 2. Abba

_____ 3. the Lord's Prayer

_____ 4. the Our Father

_____ 5. private prayer

_____ 6. public prayer

Column B

a. The prayer Jesus gave us

b. Praying alone

c. Praying with others

d. Talking and listening to God

e. A word that means "father"

f. Another name for the Lord's Prayer

Answer the following questions.

1. How did Jesus show his trust in his Father?

_____

2. Why do we trust God as our Father?

_____

3. What is the greatest public prayer of the Church?

_____

Think and share with your family.

Why is it important for our family to pray?

Visit our web site at www.FaithFirst.com

We Are People of Prayer

Holy, holy, holy Lord,
God of power
and might,
heaven and earth
are full of your glory.

*From the
Order of the Mass*

As people of prayer, we bless God and ask God's blessing on ourselves and others. We thank and praise God for the gifts he has given us. When do you pray?

God's blessings are all around us.

Faith Focus

What do we call the two kinds of prayers in which we ask God for help?

Faith Vocabulary

prayers of petition
Prayers of petition are prayers in which we ask God to help us.

prayers of intercession
Prayers of intercession are prayers in which we ask God to help others.

Think about times when you pray. What are some of the things you say to God when you pray? Do you ask God to give you something? Do you ask God to help someone out?

We Ask God for Help

Jesus taught us to ask God for all we need. One day Jesus said,

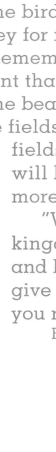

"Look at the birds in the sky. They have no money for food and yet God feeds them. Remember that you are more important than they are.

"Look at the beautiful wild flowers that cover the fields. If God clothes the fields in such beauty, will he not take even more care of you?

"Work for God's kingdom and his mercy and love. Then God will give you everything that you really need."

Based on Matthew 6:26–33

To Help You Remember

1. What is it called when we pray for others?

2. What do you ask for when you pray?

We trust God will help us. We have a special name for these prayers. We call them **prayers of petition.** Our prayers of petition are signs of our faith and trust in God.

We also pray for others. We pray that everyone may know that God loves them. We ask God to forgive and to bless everyone. We call these prayers for others **prayers of intercession.**

Praying for Others

Look carefully at the pictures. Choose one picture. Write a prayer for the person in the picture.

_____

_____

_____

_____

_____

Faith Vocabulary

prayers of blessing
Prayers of blessing are prayers in which we remember that God is the Creator of everything that is good.

"God bless you" is a prayer. When has anyone ever said that prayer to you? What were they asking from God?

We Bless God

Besides prayers of petition and intercession, we pray other kinds of prayers too. Often we pray a **prayer of blessing.** In this prayer we tell God that we believe that he is our Father and Creator.

At Mass the priest prays a special blessing prayer. He takes the plate holding the bread that will become the Body of Jesus and lifts it up. Holding it in his hands, he prays,

"Blessed are you, Lord, God of all creation. Through your goodness we have this bread to offer, which earth has given and human hands have made. It will become for us the bread of life."

We respond, "Blessed be God for ever."

The priest then holds up the cup of wine and says another prayer of blessing.

The bread and the wine are God's gifts to us. They are also our gifts to God. God blesses us, and we bless God.

To Help You Remember

1. What is a prayer of blessing?

2. Why do we bless God at Mass?

With My Family

Memorize the Grace Before Meals blessing prayer. Pray it with your family.

Blessed Be God Forever!

What are some of the things you would like to bless God for? Finish this prayer by writing those things on the lines.

Dear God,

I bless you because you have created me.

Blessed be God forever!

I bless you because _____.

Blessed be God forever!

I bless you because _____.

Blessed be God forever!

I ask your blessing on _____.

Blessed be God forever!

Amen. So it is! So it may be! Alleluia!

Faith Vocabulary

prayers of thanksgiving
Prayers of thanksgiving are prayers in which we thank God for every blessing.

prayers of praise
Prayers of praise are prayers in which we show our love and respect for God.

Have you ever whispered, "Thanks, God!" when something good happened to you? Jesus teaches us that this kind of prayer is one of the most important kinds of prayer.

We Thank God

Jesus teaches us the importance of thanking God in this gospel story.

One day Jesus met a group of ten sick people. They all had a very serious disease called leprosy that everyone could see. Think how they felt when people stared at them or ran away from them because of their disease. Then act out the play.

GROUP: Jesus, have pity on us!

JESUS: Go and show yourselves to the religious leaders!
(All ten rush away. As they go, God heals them of their disease. Only one man hurries back. He falls down at Jesus' feet.)

THE MAN: Glory to God! I am healed! Thank you, Jesus!

JESUS: Ten were healed. Where are the other nine? Are you the only one to thank God? Go! Your faith has saved you!

Based on Luke 17:12–18

Like the man who was cured, we give thanks to God. We thank God for the blessings of our life. When we do this, we are praying a **prayer of thanksgiving.**

We also pray **prayers of praise.** We praise God for the mighty deeds of creation. We praise God for the gift of Jesus. We praise God for the blessings of our world and our life. When we praise God, we show him our love and respect.

To Help You Remember

1. In the gospel story, how many people who were healed remembered to thank God?

2. Why do we thank and praise God?

Praising God

Add your own praise to the following psalm of praise.

Praise God, sun and moon!

Praise God, all shining stars!

Praise God, _____.

Praise God, _____.

Praise God, _____.

Praise God, _____.

Amen. So it is! So it may be! Alleluia!

We pray prayers of petition, intercession, blessing, thanksgiving, and praise.

We Are People of Prayer

Many parishes have prayer groups. Parishioners gather at the parish church or in homes to read the Scriptures and to pray together. They ask God's help for themselves and others. They bless God and ask God's blessing. Together they pray prayers of praise and thanks.

Parish prayer groups are a sign to us that we are people of prayer!

What are some of the ways the people of your parish come together to pray?

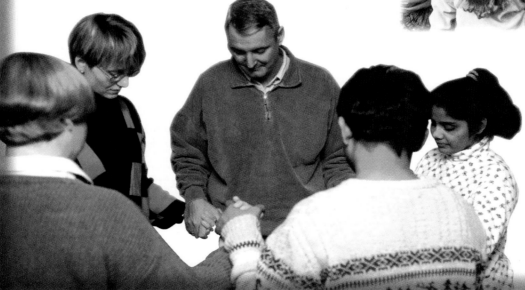

You are a person of prayer. You pray prayers of petition, intercession, blessing, praise, and thanksgiving.

Pray All Ways

Decorate this prayer poster.

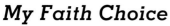

Lord, hear my prayer.

My Faith Choice

This week I will try to pray every morning and every night.

And now we pray.

It is good to give thanks to the LORD, to sing praise to your name, Most High, To proclaim your love in the morning, your faithfulness in the night.

Psalm 92:2–3

CHAPTER REVIEW

Complete each sentence.

1. When I ask God to give me something I need, this is called a prayer of p_____ .

2. When I ask God to help another person, it is called a prayer of i_____ .

3. When I thank God for all he has done for me, it is called a prayer of t_____ .

4. When I tell God how wonderful he is, it is called a prayer of p_____ .

Answer the following questions.

1. Why are we called people of prayer?

   _____

   _____

2. What is a prayer of blessing?

   _____

   _____

3. Why should we always pray prayers of thanksgiving and praise?

   _____

   _____

Think and share with your family.

How can our family members be more faithful people of prayer?

Visit our
web site at
www.FaithFirst.com

254

We Profess our Faith

25

We Pray

I believe in God,
the Father almighty,
creator of heaven
and earth.
I believe in
Jesus Christ,
his only Son,
our Lord.
I believe
in the Holy Spirit.

*Taken from the
Apostles' Creed*

We profess our faith in God by praying creeds. A creed is a statement of beliefs. What are the names of the creeds the Church prays?

Jesus invites us to place our trust in him.

Faith Focus

What does the word creed mean?

Think about those things that we believe about others. We believe that our parents love us. We believe that our friends care about us. We believe that our teachers want us to learn.

We Believe

As Christians we have many beliefs about ourselves and the people in our lives. We have beliefs about God too.

We say what we believe about God in special prayers called creeds. The word *creed* comes from two words that mean "I give my heart to it." As we pray our creed, we give our heart to God. This means we really believe what we are praying.

After Jesus was raised from the dead, he appeared to Thomas, who was an apostle. Thomas saw him and said, "My Lord and my God!"

With these few words, Thomas said that he believed Jesus was God. These words were his creed. He gave his heart to Jesus. He was saying, "I believe in you with all my heart."

256

The apostle Paul wrote one of the earliest creeds of the church community. In a letter to the Christian community in Corinth he wrote,

> I have handed on to you what I have received. Christ died for our sins. He was buried. God raised him to new life on the third day. This is what I have preached to you. This is what you must believe.

Based on 1 Corinthians 15:3–11

Paul told the early Christians what they needed to believe as followers of Jesus. His words are a creed. They are a brief statement of what the Church believes about Jesus. Since Jesus' Resurrection, the Church has given its heart to these beliefs.

To Help You Remember

1. What does the word creed mean?

2. Why do we give our heart to what we believe?

We Believe

What is one belief about God that you have given your heart to? Write a prayer that expresses your beliefs about God. Use the following outline to help you. Pray it together with your classmates.

ALL: O God, today we give our hearts to you.

1ST SPEAKER: We believe in _____ .

ALL: We give our hearts to you.

2ND SPEAKER: We believe in _____ .

ALL: We give our hearts to you.

3RD SPEAKER: We believe in _____ .

ALL: We give our hearts to you.
Amen.

proclaim
To say aloud with the community is to proclaim.

Apostles' Creed
The Apostles' Creed is one of the main creeds of the Catholic Church.

The Apostles' Creed

Decorate the border around the Apostles' Creed to help you learn it. Use some of the words from the creed as part of your decoration.

Each of us has our own beliefs. Families have beliefs too. What is something your family believes about life, people, or God?

We Pray the Apostles' Creed

Our church family shares its beliefs with us too. One way it does this is when we **proclaim** those beliefs by praying the **Apostles' Creed.**

The Apostles' Creed is one of the main creeds of the Church. This creed names what the Church has believed from the time of the apostles.

The Apostles' Creed

1. *I believe in God, the Father almighty, creator of heaven and earth.*

2. *I believe in Jesus Christ, his only Son, our Lord.*

3. *He was conceived by the power of the Holy Spirit and born of the Virgin Mary.*

4. *He suffered under Pontius Pilate, was crucified, died, and was buried. He descended to the dead.*

As a church community, it is important to proclaim our beliefs together. This helps us to never forget why we are a Christian community. Sharing our beliefs about God, Jesus, the Holy Spirit, and the Church helps make us a united family.

The Apostles' Creed names seven important beliefs of our church family.

To Help You Remember

1. What does the Apostles' Creed express?

2. Why do we proclaim this creed as a community of believers?

With My Family

Memorize the Apostles' Creed and pray it with your family.

5. *On the third day he rose again.*

6. *He ascended into heaven and is seated at the right hand of the Father. He will come again to judge the living and the dead.*

7. *I believe in the Holy Spirit, the holy catholic Church, the communion of saints, the forgiveness of sins, the resurrection of the body, and the life everlasting. Amen.*

Everyone learns how to pray from others. Who taught you how to pray?

The Holy Spirit Helps Us to Pray

Many people teach us to pray. Priests are called to teach others how to pray by their example and by their words. Families and teachers teach us to pray too.

Learning how to pray is one of the most important things we learn as Catholics.

Jesus knew that his followers would need help to pray. Before he died, Jesus explained who would help them to pray when he was gone from their eyes. He said,

"The Holy Spirit will be with you always. The Spirit will teach you everything. The Spirit will remind you of all that I have told you."

Based on John 14:16, 26

The most important One who teaches us to pray is the Holy Spirit. In the New Testament we read,

We do not know how to pray as we ought. The Spirit who knows what is in our hearts helps us.

Based on Romans 8:26

As Christians we believe this with all our heart. We pray this prayer to show our faith and trust in the Holy Spirit.

Come, Holy Spirit,
    fill our hearts
    with your love.

Every moment of every day, the Holy Spirit helps us. The Spirit helps us pray. When we cannot pray, the Holy Spirit prays for us. The Holy Spirit is always praying in us and through us.

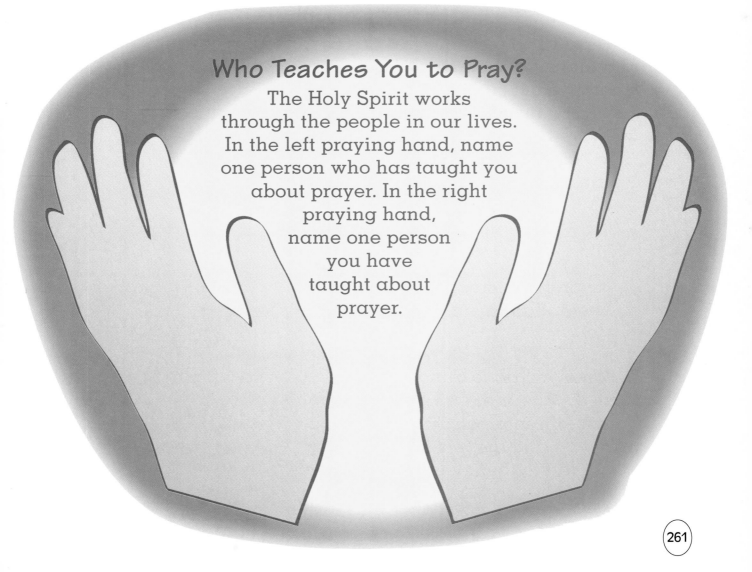

Who Teaches You to Pray?

The Holy Spirit works through the people in our lives. In the left praying hand, name one person who has taught you about prayer. In the right praying hand, name one person you have taught about prayer.

Praying the creed is a sign we are giving our heart to God. We are saying we believe all that he has revealed, or made known, to us.

The Nicene Creed

The Apostles' Creed is one of the important creeds of our Church. Another important creed is called the Nicene Creed. The Nicene Creed is much longer than the Apostles' Creed. This is the creed we most often pray at Sunday Mass.

We also profess, or pray, a creed at Baptism. At Baptism we pray our creed in a special way. The priest or deacon asks us questions about what we believe, and we respond, "I do." Here is an example.

Priest: Do you believe in God,
           the Father almighty,
           creator of heaven and earth?

All: I do.

We pray the creed this way on Easter Sunday too.

When you go to Sunday Mass, listen for the Nicene Creed. Join in proclaiming what you and the rest of your parish family believes.

We believe in one God, the Father, the Almighty.

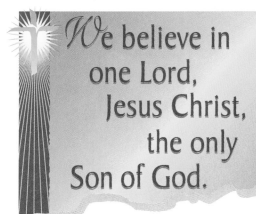

We believe in one Lord, Jesus Christ, the only Son of God.

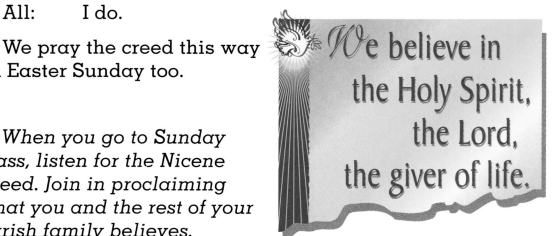

We believe in the Holy Spirit, the Lord, the giver of life.

You belong to the community of the Catholic Church. Knowing what you believe as a Catholic is very important. What you believe as a Catholic helps you live as a follower of Jesus. It helps you share with others what God has made known to us about himself and his love for us.

We Believe

Design a poster that tells who you are and what you believe as a Catholic Christian.

My Faith Choice

This week I will pray the _____ Creed alone or with others. I will think about what this prayer teaches me about God.

And now we pray.

Come, Holy Spirit, fill our hearts with your love.

CHAPTER REVIEW

Match the words in column A with their definitions in column B.

Column A

_____ 1. creed

_____ 2. Apostles' Creed

_____ 3. Holy Spirit

_____ 4. Jesus

Column B

a. Promised to send the Holy Spirit to help us pray

b. A collection of statements that tell what we believe about God

c. The Helper who prays in us and helps us to pray

d. The creed that names what the Church has believed from the days of the apostles

Answer the following questions.

1. What does the word *creed* mean?

_____

2. What does the word *creed* tell us we are doing when we pray a creed?

_____

3. How does the Holy Spirit help us to pray?

_____

Think and share with your family.

What does it mean for the members of your family to give their hearts to God?

Visit our web site at www.FaithFirst.com

The Hail Mary
A Scripture Story

26

Hail Mary,
full of grace,
the Lord is with you!
Blessed are you
among women,
and blessed
is the fruit
of your womb, Jesus.
From the Hail Mary

When we pray the Hail Mary, we ask Mary to pray for us. Where did the Church get the words for the Hail Mary?

"Mary, most blessed are you among women."
Based on Luke 1:42

Bible Background

Women in the Bible have always been leaders in answering God's call.

Jewish Women

Long ago Jewish women made their own clothing and blankets for their families. They made bread and carried water from the village well. They made sure to have enough oil for the lamps used in their homes.

At that time Jewish girls learned about their religion and the customs of their people in their homes. They learned about the Scriptures and the Law of Moses mostly at home. When they became mothers, they taught the Law to their children.

From listening to the Scriptures of God's chosen people, they came to know the stories about Hannah, Sarah, Ruth, Esther, and other faith-filled women.

They also learned that God had promised to send a savior to his people. This Savior came to be called the Messiah, God's Promised One who would show them how to live.

A Young Woman in Nazareth

All the young Jewish women waited in expectation. One of them would be the mother of the Messiah. Who would it be?

One young Jewish woman lived in the town of **Nazareth** in Galilee. This humble young woman knew the Jewish Scriptures. She listened to the stories of God's promises to his people.

Daily she did her chores around the house. She prayed and worked and slept. Like all her people, she waited for the Messiah. This young woman's Jewish name was Mary, which means "excellence."

To Help You Remember

1. How did Jewish women who lived in Jesus' time learn the stories of their religion?

2. How did they learn about God's promise to send a savior?

In Mary's Time

Imagine that you lived long ago in the land where Jesus was born. You are a newspaper reporter. Write three questions you would ask a young Jewish woman. Then choose a partner and ask your partner the questions. Record the answers.

Question 1: _____

_____

Question 2: _____

_____

Question 3: _____

_____

Reading the Word of God

Faith Focus

What did God ask of Mary?

When we meet a friend, we say, "Hello!" When our friend says something important, we really listen. One day a woman named Mary really listened when an angel said "Hello!" to her.

Stained-glass window of the angel Gabriel greeting Mary.

The Annunciation

The humble young woman named Mary did not expect to meet an angel. But that is what happened. Here is the story.

God sent the angel Gabriel to a town in Galilee called Nazareth. The angel came to the home of a young woman named Mary. The angel greeted her by saying, "Hail, you are full of grace, for God is with you."

Then the angel said, "Do not be afraid, Mary. God loves you. Behold, you shall have a son. You will name him Jesus. He will be great. He will be the Son of God."

Then the angel told Mary something else. The angel said, "Elizabeth, your relative, will bear a son too."

Mary said, "I am God's servant. May all that you have said be done according to God's word."

Then the angel left. Mary left Nazareth and went to visit Elizabeth.

When Elizabeth saw Mary, she said, "Blessed are you among women, and blessed is the child you carry within your womb."

Based on Luke 1:26–42

To Help You Remember

1. What did the angel tell Mary?

2. What was Mary's answer to God?

The Angel's Announcement

Write a play about the Annunciation and Mary's visit to Elizabeth. Present your play to the class. On the lines provided, write the first words of your play.

_____

_____

_____

_____

_____

_____

_____

_____

Understanding the Word of God

Faith Focus

How does the Church use the angel's greeting to Mary?

Faith Vocabulary

Hail Mary

Hail Mary is a prayer based on the angel Gabriel's greeting to Mary at the Annunciation.

honor

Honor means "to show respect and love for someone."

ail Mary, full of grace, the Lord is with you! Blessed are you among women, and blessed is the fruit of your womb, Jesus. Holy Mary, Mother of God, pray for us sinners, now and at the hour of our death. Amen.

Mary and Elizabeth must have talked about what the angel Gabriel said. Mary stored the words in her mind and heart. The Church too remembers these words. We use them in prayer.

The Angel's Words

The angel greeted Mary by saying "Hail," or "Hello." Then the angel told Mary that God was with her in a special way. She was full of grace. God's life and love lived in her.

When Mary visited Elizabeth, Elizabeth said that Mary was blessed. God had given Mary the great gift of her son, Jesus.

270

The Hail Mary

The Church uses the words of Gabriel and Elizabeth to pray to Mary. We call this prayer the **Hail Mary.**

The first two lines of the prayer are the words of the angel Gabriel. The words of Elizabeth are the next two lines.

The Church has added the second part of the prayer. With these words we **honor** Mary. We ask her to help us be full of faith just as she was.

Mary shows us how to say yes to God. We honor Mary for her great faith. We show our honor by praying the Hail Mary.

To Help You Remember

1. According to the Bible, who said the first two lines of the Hail Mary?

2. What do the words of the second part of the Hail Mary mean?

With My Family

Say the Hail Mary with your family before you go someplace together this week.

Showing Our Love for Mary

Many years ago monks decorated the Bible with pictures and beautiful colors. This showed their love for God. Decorate these letters to show your love for Mary.

H ail M ary

Mary said yes to God and became the mother of Jesus. Throughout her whole life, she loved God.

We Pray the Rosary

The Church has always honored Mary. One way we show that Mary is special to us is by praying the rosary. The rosary consists of five decades, or sets of ten, Hail Marys. Each decade begins with the Lord's Prayer and ends with the Glory Prayer.

Usually we pray the rosary on a string of beads. The string of beads is connected to a crucifix. As we pray each decade of the rosary, we remember an event, or mystery, in the life of Jesus and Mary.

The Joyful Mysteries help us to remember the early life of Jesus and Mary. The Sorrowful Mysteries help us to remember Jesus' death. The Glorious Mysteries help us to remember that God raised Jesus to new life.

How do you honor Mary?

What Difference Does It Make in My Life?

Repeating the Hail Mary as we pray the rosary helps us to remember that Mary believed in God's love. Because of her faith she was able to say yes to God.

Saying Yes to God

It is not always easy for us to say yes to God. Think of a time when you might find it hard to do what God is calling you to do. Write a prayer asking Mary to help you say yes to God.

____

____

____

____

____

____

____

____

My Faith Choice

This week I will pray the Hail Mary when

______________________________ .

This week I will say, "Yes!" to God when

______________________________ .

And now we pray.

Hail Mary, full of grace, the Lord is with you!

Based on Luke 1:28

Write *True* or *False* next to each sentence.

1. The Our Father is the most well-known prayer to Mary. _____

2. Some of the words of the Hail Mary come from the gospel stories of the Annunciation and the Visitation. _____

3. When we honor someone, we show them that they are special. _____

4. A role model is someone we want to be like. _____

5. The rosary is a prayer we pray to honor Mary. _____

Answer the following questions.

1. What do you think the angel Gabriel's words meant to Mary?_____

_____

_____

2. Why do we honor Mary? _____

_____

_____

_____

Think and share with your family.

Read Luke 2:26–45 together as a family. Then talk about what the story means to each of you.

Visit our web site at www.FaithFirst.com

We Celebrate
The Liturgical Seasons

The Liturgical Year/Ordinary Time

Faith Focus

How do we celebrate our faith all year long?

The Word of the Lord

Choose this year's gospel reading for the Sixteenth Sunday in Ordinary Time. Read and discuss it with your family.

Year A:
   Matthew 13:24-43

Year B:
   Mark 6:30-34

Year C:
   Luke 10:38-42

Certain programs that you watch on TV are on at prime time. That is the special time when most children and adults watch their favorite shows, usually after dinner and before bedtime.

Seasons of the Church Year

We can think of the special church seasons as prime times. They are times of preparation and celebration.

The seasons in the church year are Advent, Christmas, Lent, and Easter. All the other times are called Ordinary Time. Ordinary Time is the longest time in the church year.

Each week of the year we gather at Mass to celebrate and pray. We listen to the Scripture readings to hear God's message to us. We hear about Jesus and what he taught us by his words and actions.

Each of the church seasons has a special color. During Advent and Lent the color purple or violet is used. During Christmas and Easter either white or gold is used. On some days like Palm Sunday, Good Friday, and Pentecost the color red is used. Green is the color used during Ordinary Time.

To Help You Remember

1. What are the names of the church seasons?

2. Which church season is the longest?

Name the Seasons

Use the colors gold or white, purple or violet, and green to color the stoles that the priest wears during the specific church seasons. Write the name of the season under each stole.

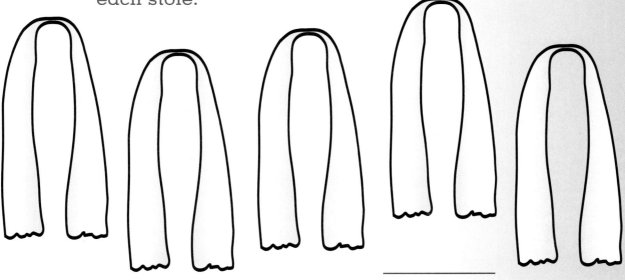

_____

_____

_____

_____

_____

What can you do to show your love for God during Ordinary Time?

_____

_____

_____

Faith Focus

Who are some of the people that prepared us for Jesus' coming?

The Word of the Lord

Choose this year's gospel reading for the First Sunday of Advent. Read and discuss it with your family.

Year A:
   Matthew 24:37-44

Year B:
   Mark 13:33-37

Year C:
   Luke 21:25-28, 34-36

What You See

The Advent wreath is made of evergreens and four candles. Each week we light another candle as we wait for the coming of Christ at Christmastime.

You know the names of your parents and grandparents and aunts and uncles. They are part of your family tree. A family tree helps you to remember the people in your family.

A Jesse Tree

During Advent we make a family tree to prepare for Christmas. It helps us to remember the people who prepared the way for Jesus.

We call this tree a Jesse tree. Jesse was a shepherd from Bethlehem. He was also the father of King David, an ancestor of Jesus. We hang symbols on the Jesse tree to remind us of the people who prepared the way for Jesus.

We remember Adam and Eve and Noah. We remember Abraham and Sarah and Moses and David.

We remember John the Baptist, who announced the coming of Jesus. We remember Mary and Joseph, who welcomed him on the first Christmas night.

To Help You Remember

1. Why do we make a Jesse tree?

2. Who were some of the people who prepared for Jesus?

Welcoming Jesus

Beside each star write the name of someone who helps you wait and prepare for the coming of Jesus at Christmas.

Faith Focus

Who was John the Baptist?

The Word of the Lord

Choose this year's gospel reading for the Second Sunday of Advent. Read and discuss it with your family.

Year A:
Matthew 3:1-12

Year B:
Mark 1:1-8

Year C:
Luke 3:1-6

Our parents and our teachers help us to get ready for big celebrations. They help us to prepare when someone comes to visit our home or classroom.

Prepare the Way!

John the Baptist helped people to prepare for the coming of Jesus. When John was born, his father said,

"And you, child, will be called prophet of the Most High,
for you will go before the Lord to prepare his ways."

Luke 1:76

When he was a young man, John lived in the desert. He learned the Scriptures of his people, the people of Israel. Then one day John came to the banks of the Jordan River. There he announced the coming of the Messiah.

John called people to prepare to receive the Messiah promised by God. Many changed their ways, and John baptized them. They waited with great hope for the Messiah. They knew he was coming soon.

Get Ready

There are _____ days until Christmas. How will you prepare for Christmas?

I can pray for

_____

by _____

_____.

I can make up with

_____

by _____

_____.

I can offer to help

_____

by _____

_____.

I can make a gift for

_____

by _____

_____.

Faith Focus
How does God speak to us?

The Word of the Lord

Choose this year's gospel reading for the Third Sunday of Advent. Read and discuss it with your family.

Year A:
Matthew 11:2-11

Year B:
John 1:6-8, 19-28

Year C:
Luke 3:10-18

The Messiah

God speaks to us in many ways. He speaks to us when people care for us. God speaks to us when people reach out to help us. God speaks his love for us through people who teach us about him.

Long ago God called forth good and holy people to speak in his name. We call these people prophets. The prophet Isaiah said that God would send them a new leader who would bring peace and justice.

The prophet Jeremiah said that God's Promised One would be a shepherd. He would do what is right and just. Micah said that he would be born in Bethlehem.

The words of the prophets came true in the birth of Jesus. As Christmas draws near, we look forward to the peace of the promised Messiah.

To Help You Remember

1. In what ways does God speak to us?

2. What is a prophet?

The Lord Is Near

Here is a prayer you and your family may use as Christmas draws near.

As we wait for the coming of Jesus, let us also prepare to welcome him.

To welcome Jesus we will

say welcome

You are near to us. We rejoice in you.

To show our joy that Jesus is near, we will

be happy

You are near to us. We offer our prayer to you.

Our prayer is

Holy Mary

You are near to us. We wait in patient hope.

Amen.

Faith Focus

How do we prepare for Jesus?

Stained-glass window of Mary and Elizabeth.

The Word of the Lord

Choose this year's gospel reading for the Fourth Sunday of Advent. Read and discuss it with your family.

Year A:
Matthew 1:18-24

Year B:
Luke 1:26-38

Year C:
Luke 1:39-45

We know how to get ready to celebrate a birthday. We may decorate the house. We may bake a cake. We may wrap gifts. We may even plan a favorite meal.

All Is Ready

During the last days of Advent, we prepare our hearts to welcome Jesus. The Church invites us to read the stories of the family of Jesus. We read about the angel who announced the news of Jesus' birth to Mary. The angel said, "Hail, favored one! The Lord is with you" (Luke 1:28).

Mary went to visit her cousin, Elizabeth. She said to Mary, "Most blessed are you among women" (Luke 1:42).

An angel helped Joseph to understand that Mary's child would save all people from their sins. The angel asked Joseph to take care of Mary. Joseph said yes, and he took her into his home.

To Help You Remember

1. What happened to prepare Mary and Joseph for Jesus' birth?

2. How does the Church ask us to prepare for the coming of Jesus?

We Are Ready

READER 1: Isaiah the prophet said, "The virgin shall be with child, and bear a son, and shall name him Immanuel" (Isaiah 7:14).

ALL: We are ready!

READER 2: Mary said, "Behold, I am the handmaid of the Lord. May it be done to me according to your word" (Luke 1:38). Mary was ready.

ALL: We are ready!

READER 3: Elizabeth said of Mary, "Most blessed are you among women" (Luke 1:42). Elizabeth was ready.

ALL: We are ready!

READER 4: Paul said to us, "Rejoice in the Lord always. I shall say it again: rejoice! Your kindness should be known to all. The Lord is near" (Philippians 4:4–5).

ALL: We are all ready! Come, Lord Jesus!

Faith Focus

How do we celebrate the arrival of Jesus?

Stained-glass window of Jesus, Mary, and Joseph.

The Word of the Lord

Choose this year's gospel reading for the Mass on Christmas Day. Read and discuss it with your family.

John 1:1-18
    or 1:1-5, 9-14

What You See

The Nativity scene (or crèche) has a new addition. It is baby Jesus! Nativity scenes usually remain on display until the feast of the Epiphany on January 6.

Shout for Joy!

Christmas is a time to rejoice! When Jesus was born, angels and shepherds rejoiced. The Masses for Christmas Day invite us to rejoice too.

We use all creation to help us rejoice. We decorate bread and cookies. We wrap packages. We put lights on our trees. We want the whole earth to rejoice and be glad. We want heaven and nature to sing.

In Psalm 96 we read that the trees of the forest shout with joy. The prophet Isaiah says that all creatures will happily live with one another.

The wolf shall be a guest
    of the lamb.
The calf and the young lion shall
    browse together,
      with a little child to guide them.

Isaiah 11:6

The whole world celebrates the birth of the newborn king. He has made everything new again.

To Help You Remember

1. How do we use creation to help us rejoice?

2. What does the prophet Isaiah say about the world now that Jesus is here?

A Blessing for Trees

Here is a prayer you and your family may use to bless a Christmas tree.

LEADER: Our help is in the name of the Lord.

ALL: Who made heaven and earth.

READER 1: Sing to the Lord a new song. Sing to the Lord, all the earth. Bless his name; announce his salvation day after day.

ALL: Sing to the Lord a new song.

READER 2: Let the heavens be glad and the earth rejoice; let the sea and what fills it resound; let the plains be joyful and all that is in them.

ALL: Sing to the Lord a new song.

READER 3: Then let all the trees of the forest rejoice before the Lord who comes, who comes to govern the earth.

LEADER: As you hold up your evergreen boughs, let us pray:

O Lord, bless this bough and all the trees of the forest. Let them shine with light and snow. May their green life remind us of eternal life. May their decorations celebrate your coming among us. We ask this in the name of Jesus your Son, born of the Virgin for us.

ALL: Amen.

Based on Psalm 96

Faith Focus

Why do we call Jesus our Savior?

The Word of the Lord

This is the second reading for the Second Sunday of Christmas. Read and discuss it with your family.

Ephesians 1:3-6, 15-18

What You Hear

When we celebrate Jesus' birth, you often hear the word *Alleluia* in songs we sing. *Alleluia* means "Praise God." We sing praise to God for sending his Son, Jesus who saves us from sin. In doing this, he is our salvation.

Jesus Our Savior

During Christmastime we give and receive gifts. We feel happy because God's Promised One is with us. Jesus has come to be our Savior. The name *Jesus* means "God saves."

The angel Gabriel told Mary that she would bear God's Son. His name would be Jesus because he would save his people from their sins. Later, shepherds heard angels announce that a savior was born in Bethlehem. Some wise men, called magi, brought gifts to the Savior.

When Mary and Joseph brought Jesus to the Temple, Simeon and Anna rejoiced. Simeon blessed the child. He praised God and said,

> "My eyes have seen your salvation."
> Luke 2:30

During Christmas the Church honors Jesus as our Savior. We remember that Jesus' birth is part of the great mystery of salvation.

To Help You Remember

1. Why was *Jesus* chosen as the baby's name?

2. What kind of gifts could you give others that honor Jesus?

Celebrating the Birth of Jesus

Write a poem by following the steps below.

Line 1: one word telling about Jesus

Line 2: the names of Jesus' mother and foster-father

Line 3: three other names for Jesus

Line 4: two words about the first Christmas night

Line 5: one word about your Christmas celebration

Jesus

helps

Mary joseph

Father son holy spirit

_____ _____

happy

Faith Focus

How do we spend our time during Lent?

The Word of the Lord

Choose this year's gospel reading for the First Sunday of Lent. Read and discuss it with your family.

Year A:
  Matthew 4:1-11

Year B:
  Mark 1:12-15

Year C:
  Luke 4:1-13

Think of a wonderful thing that will happen soon in your life. Will you celebrate your birthday? Will you go on a trip? Will you see a friend again? What will you do to prepare for this event?

Lent

During the season of Lent we prepare for a wonderful happening. We get ready for Easter. We try extra hard to give time and effort to help others. We also fast, or give up something, and we try to pray more.

During Lent we try to become more like Jesus. Giving time and effort, giving up something, and praying better are three ways we become more like Jesus.

The Church gathers us to work and pray together during Lent. The Church encourages us to give, to fast, and to pray. In these ways we prepare for the wonderful celebration of Easter.

On the Way to Easter

Check the things in each box that you will do during Lent to prepare for Easter.

To Help You Remember

1. What are three ways we try to become more like Jesus during Lent?

2. What are some ways you would like to become more like Jesus?

I will give

____ a smile to someone who looks sad.

____ kind words to someone who loves me.

____ help to someone in need.

____ thanks to someone who has helped me.

____ other _____.

I will give up

____ a snack during the day.

____ a favorite TV show.

____ arguing.

____ a bad habit.

____ other _____.

I will pray for

_____.

_____.

_____.

_____.

Faith Focus

What does it mean to be a "cheerful giver"?

The Word of the Lord

Choose this year's gospel reading for the Second Sunday of Lent. Read and discuss it with your family.

Year A:
  Matthew 17:1-9

Year B:
  Mark 9:2-10

Year C:
  Luke 9:28-36

Sometimes we have to do hard things. We may have to give time to our younger brother or sister when we would like to play with friends. We may have to give something away that we want to keep. At these times it is not always easy to be cheerful.

A Cheerful Giver

During Lent we give time away. We give up things and pray. Jesus asks us to be quiet and cheerful givers. He teaches us to give away money and goods without telling everyone about our good deeds. The apostle Paul adds to this idea. He tells us, "God loves a cheerful giver" (2 Corinthians 9:7).

Jesus also asks us to fast, or give up things. He wants us to be bright and cheerful when we do this. When we fast without looking gloomy, we follow Jesus.

Jesus also asks us to pray simply and confidently to God. We pray from the deepest part of our heart. Jesus reminds us that God, our Father, knows our needs.

To Help You Remember

1. What does Jesus teach us about giving during Lent?

2. How do we pray during Lent?

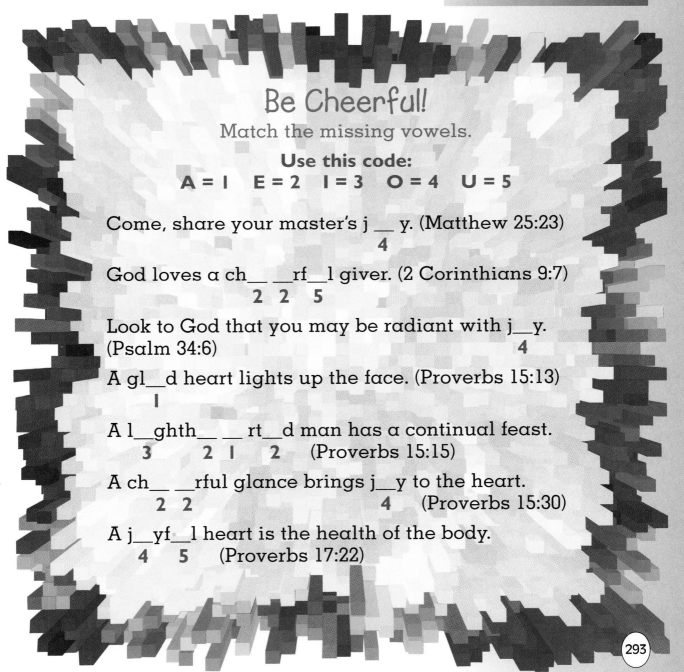

Be Cheerful!

Match the missing vowels.

Use this code:

A = 1   E = 2   I = 3   O = 4   U = 5

Come, share your master's j __ y. (Matthew 25:23)
             4

God loves a ch__ __rf__l giver. (2 Corinthians 9:7)
            2 2   5

Look to God that you may be radiant with j__y.
(Psalm 34:6)   4

A gl__d heart lights up the face. (Proverbs 15:13)
    1

A l__ghth__ __ rt__d man has a continual feast.
    3   2 1   2   (Proverbs 15:15)

A ch__ __rful glance brings j__y to the heart.
    2 2   4   (Proverbs 15:30)

A j__yf__l heart is the health of the body.
    4   5   (Proverbs 17:22)

Faith Focus

How do we know God is near?

The Word of the Lord

Choose this year's gospel reading for the Third Sunday of Lent. Read and discuss it with your family.

Year A:
John 4:5-42 or
John 4:5-15, 19-26, 39, 40-44

Year B:
John 2:13-25

Year C:
Luke 13:1-9

What You Hear

During Lent you will not hear our Church sing the Alleluia. This is because we will not rejoice until we celebrate Jesus being raised from the dead on Easter.

Praying Alone and Together

We like to talk to our friends, but sometimes they are too busy. God is never too busy. God is one friend we can always talk to. We can thank and praise God and tell him our needs anytime and anywhere.

Faith tells us that God is always near. Prayer helps us to be aware that God is near. Psalm 37:7 tells us, "Be still before the LORD; wait for God." During Lent we ask God to draw near us.

We are a people of prayer. On Sunday we gather to give praise and thanks to God. The Eucharist is our shared prayer to God. When we pray together, we celebrate our friendship with God.

During Lent we also pray alone. In the silence of our heart, we pray to God. When we pray alone, we celebrate our friendship with God.

To Help You Remember

1. What are we doing when we pray together and alone?

2. Where are your favorite places to pray together? Alone?

You Are Here

Create the second verse to this prayer-song. Sing it to the tune of "Kumbaya."

Verse 1
    Someone's praying, Lord,
    The Lord is near.
    Someone's praying, Lord,
    The Lord is near.
    Someone's praying, Lord,
    The Lord is near.
    O Lord, you are near.

Verse 2
    Someone's _____ , Lord,
    You are here.
    Someone's _____ , Lord,
    You are here.
    Someone's _____ , Lord,
    You are here.
    O Lord, you are here.

Faith Focus

How does Jesus want us to help people?

The Word of the Lord

Choose this year's gospel reading for the Fourth Sunday of Lent. Read and discuss it with your family.

Year A:
John 9:1-41 or
John 9:1, 6-9, 13-17, 34-38

Year B:
John 3:14-21

Year C:
Luke 15:1-3, 11-32

Sometimes we see people who need our help. But we do not take the time to help. Helping does not seem important to us at that time. "Someone else will help," we say.

A Time to Give

Jesus asks us to care for everyone. He wants us to care for people who seem unimportant to others.

Jesus said that when we care about these people, we care for him. When we feed someone who is hungry, we feed Jesus. When someone is thirsty and we offer them a drink, we offer Jesus a drink. When someone is alone or imprisoned and we visit them, we visit Jesus.

During Lent we think of ways to give to those who need help. We remember that even the smallest things we do for those in need really do make a difference.

To Help You Remember

1. What does Jesus ask of us?

2. What are some things we can do to care for Jesus?

Martin and the Beggar

Read this story. Write the ending yourself.

Once upon a time, Martin the soldier came upon a cold, shivering beggar on the side of the road.

Martin reined in his horse and drew his sword. He cut his wool cloak in two and gave half to the beggar.

The beggar wrapped himself in the warm cloak. He grew warm with joy and happiness.

That night Martin dreamed that Jesus stood before him on the roadway, wrapped in the part of the warm cloak Martin had given away.

Suddenly, Martin knew that

_____

_____

_____ .

Hint: Read Matthew 25:35–40.

Faith Focus

Why is it important to forgive?

The Word of the Lord

Choose this year's gospel reading for the Fifth Sunday of Lent. Read and discuss it with your family.

Year A:
John 11:1-45 or
John 11:3-7, 17, 20-27, 33-45

Year B:
John 12:20-33

Year C:
John 8:1-11

Sometimes a friend hurts our feelings. Forgiving that friend can be difficult. But Jesus asks us to forgive others just as God forgives us. Jesus shows us that God is always ready to forgive. We must always be ready to forgive also.

Be Reconciled

Sometimes we turn away from God and hurt others. At these times we need forgiveness. When we fail, God seeks us the way a shepherd seeks lost sheep. God rejoices like a woman who finds a lost coin. God welcomes us home the way a father welcomes his wandering child.

During Lent the Church invites us to celebrate God's forgiveness. The Church encourages us to celebrate our return to God through the sacrament of Reconciliation.

When we have been lost and alone, God rejoices at our return. God welcomes us back. We find peace with God and with one another.

To Help You Remember

1. When do we need forgiveness?

2. How do we celebrate God's forgiveness?

Lost and Found

LEADER: Jesus teaches us that no sin is too big for God's forgiveness.

LEADER: (Read Luke 15:8–10.)

READER 1: God has given us a world to care for. For wasting or misusing God's gift of creation,

ALL: We ask forgiveness.

READER 2: God has given us friends to help and be with us. For failing to be fair and friendly in return,

ALL: We ask forgiveness.

READER 3: God has given us grown-ups to teach and guide us. For failing to honor and obey them,

ALL: We ask forgiveness.

READER 4: God has given us tools and toys for work and play. For failing to use them with care and thankfulness,

ALL: We ask forgiveness.

LEADER: O Lord, we know you forgive us. Help us to forgive others from our heart. Keep us free from sin and evil. Lead us to the joy of your kingdom, where you live and reign forever.

ALL: Amen.

Palm Sunday of the Lord's Passion

Faith Focus

What event do we remember on Palm Sunday of the Lord's Passion?

The Word of the Lord

Choose this year's gospel reading for Palm Sunday of the Lord's Passion. Read and discuss it with your family.

Year A:
   Matthew 26:14–27:66 or 27:11–54

Year B:
   Mark 14:1–15:47 or 15:1–39

Year C:
   Luke 22:14–23:56 or 23:1–49

What You See

Palm branches are held high during the reading of the Passion of Our Lord. We do this to recreate and remember Jesus' entry into Jerusalem.

When someone important comes to your school, you celebrate. You greet the person and do special things. Many years ago children welcomed Jesus to Jerusalem. They did this on the day we call Palm Sunday of the Lord's Passion.

Hosanna!

Holy Week begins with Palm Sunday of the Lord's Passion. On that day we carry palms and remember the day Jesus came to the city of Jerusalem.

People welcomed him and cheered. They called out, "Hosanna!" They waved palm branches. They spread their cloaks on the road to make the path smooth and less dusty for Jesus.

Long ago Zechariah, a prophet, announced that a savior would come into Jerusalem just as Jesus did. The great welcome given to Jesus reminds us that he is King and Savior of all.

To Help You Remember

1. What does the great welcome on Palm Sunday of the Lord's Passion remind us about Jesus?

2. How can you be a welcoming person in your home? At school?

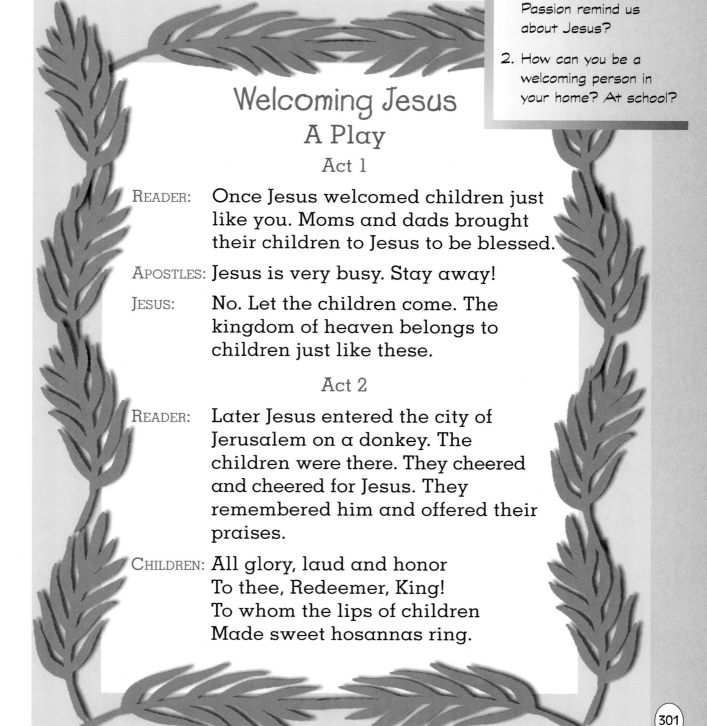

Welcoming Jesus
A Play
Act 1

READER: Once Jesus welcomed children just like you. Moms and dads brought their children to Jesus to be blessed.

APOSTLES: Jesus is very busy. Stay away!

JESUS: No. Let the children come. The kingdom of heaven belongs to children just like these.

Act 2

READER: Later Jesus entered the city of Jerusalem on a donkey. The children were there. They cheered and cheered for Jesus. They remembered him and offered their praises.

CHILDREN: All glory, laud and honor
To thee, Redeemer, King!
To whom the lips of children
Made sweet hosannas ring.

Faith Focus

What do we celebrate at the Mass of the Lord's Supper?

The Word of the Lord

Choose one of the Scripture readings for Holy Thursday. Read and discuss it with your family.

Reading I:
   Exodus 12:1–8, 11–14

Reading II:
   1 Corinthians 11:23-26

Gospel:
   John 13:1-15

Members of a team say and do special things. Members of the Church say and do special things too. We serve others just as Jesus did. We also celebrate together.

We Are Called to Serve

The celebration on Holy Thursday is called the Mass of the Lord's Supper. The Church remembers the first time Jesus took bread and wine and said, "This is my body," and "This is my blood."

Catholic churches throughout the world celebrate only one Mass on Holy Thursday. We gather around the table of the Lord. The gospel reading tells us how Jesus washed the feet of his disciples.

Stained-glass window of the Last Supper.

The washing of the disciples' feet shows us that Jesus served others. All of us who share in the Body and Blood of Christ Jesus also serve others.

To Help You Remember

1. What does the gospel reading on Holy Thursday tell us?

2. How can we serve others just as Jesus did?

Hands to Serve

Trace an outline of your hand over the words on this page. Think of ways to serve using your hands. Write them in the lines provided. Then say this prayer together.

READER 1: **When my hands comfort others,**

ALL: God is truly here.

READER 2: **When my hands carry burdens,**

ALL: God is truly here.

READER 3: **When my hands open and close in prayer,**

ALL: God is truly here.

READER 4: **When my hands hold on tight,**

ALL: God is truly here.

READER 5: _____

_____ ,

ALL: God is truly here.

READER 6: _____

_____ ,

ALL: God is truly here.

Faith Focus

Why do we remember Good Friday?

The Word of the Lord

Choose one of the Scripture readings for Good Friday. Read and discuss it with your family.

Reading I:
    Isaiah 52:13-53:12

Reading II:
    Hebrews 4:14-16; 5:7-9

Gospel:
    John 18:1-19:42

We Remember

On Good Friday we remember that Jesus died on the cross because he loved all of us. When someone is put to death on a cross, it is called a crucifixion.

Jesus was accused of being a criminal. Even though he was innocent, the people wanted him to die on the cross anyway. They shouted, "Crucify him!" The soldiers took Jesus away. They made Jesus carry his cross along the road to the place where criminals were put to death.

Before Jesus died, he forgave the people who hurt him. He asked his Father to forgive them. He prayed, "Father, forgive them for they know not what they do" (based on Luke 23:34).

Whenever we see a cross or a crucifix, we thank God for loving us so much. We also remember to forgive those who have hurt us.

To Help You Remember

1. What is the Crucifixion?

2. How did Jesus prove his love for us?

Reminders of God's Love

Write or draw something you can do this Good Friday to thank Jesus for giving his life for you.

Faith Focus

Why are Christians especially happy at Easter?

The Word of the Lord

Choose this year's gospel reading for Easter Sunday. Read and discuss it with your family.

Year A:
    John 20:1-9 or
    Matthew 28:1-10 or
    Luke 24:13-35

Year B:
    John 20:1-9 or
    Mark 16:1-7 or
    Luke 24:13-35

Year C:
    John 20:1-9 or
    Luke 24:1-12 or
    Luke 24:13-35

Praise the Lord!

Think of a time when something wonderful happened and you were really happy. Did you want to sing or shout or jump for joy? What happy words came to you? For Christians, *Alleluia* is a happy word.

We are Easter people. Alleluia is our song. We are people of the Resurrection.

Every Sunday we praise and thank God for the new life of the Resurrection. The Responsorial Psalm sung on Easter reminds us, "This is the day the Lord has made; let us be glad and rejoice in it."

During the 50 days of the Easter season, the Church sings Alleluia over and over. *Alleluia* means "Praise the Lord!" We praise God because we are new in the Lord. We walk in the light of the new day of the Resurrection.

Alleluia!

Divide your class into two groups. Face each other and take turns praying the verses of this psalm.

All: Alleluia!

1: Praise the LORD from the heavens;
    give praise in the heights.

2: Praise him, all you 〔angels〕;
    give praise, all you hosts.

1: Praise him, 〔sun〕 and 〔moon〕;
    give praise, all shining 〔stars〕.

1: You 〔lightning〕 and hail, 〔snow〕 and 〔clouds〕,
    storm winds that fulfill his command;

2: You 〔mountains〕 and all hills,
    fruit 〔trees〕 and all cedars;

1: You 〔animals〕 wild and tame.
    You kings of the 〔earth〕 and all 〔peoples〕.

All: Praise the LORD. Alleluia!   Based on Psalm 148:1–3, 7–11

To Help You Remember

1. What does the word *alleluia* mean?

2. How can you praise the Lord in a special way at Easter?

307

Faith Focus

What did the first witnesses of the Resurrection tell us about Jesus?

The Word of the Lord

The gospel reading for the Second Sunday of Easter is John 20:19-31. Read and discuss it with your family.

What You See

One of the Easter symbols is the Paschal, or Easter, candle. It is lighted at the Easter Vigil and throughout the Easter season.

Witnesses

When we witness something, we tell other people what we have seen. Many people witnessed the new life of Jesus. They told others about the Risen Lord. During the Easter season the gospel readings tell us about Jesus and the first witnesses of the Resurrection.

Mary Magdalene saw Jesus and proclaimed the good news to the disciples: "I have seen the Lord" (John 20:18). Cleopas and another disciple knew the Risen Lord in the breaking of the bread.

Jesus appeared to his apostles and gave them peace and the gift of the Holy Spirit. Thomas professed his faith in Jesus as his Lord and God.

These witnesses believed in Jesus as the Risen Lord. They were the first witnesses. By what you say and do, you are also a witness to the Risen Lord today.

To Help You Remember

1. Who are some of the first witnesses of the Resurrection?

2. How can you be a witness to the Risen Lord today?

Today's Witnesses

Mary Magdalene and Thomas were good witnesses to the Risen Lord. Draw a picture of how you can be a witness to the Risen Lord.

Faith Focus

How does Jesus ask us to serve others?

The Word of the Lord

Choose this year's gospel reading for the Third Sunday of Easter. Read and discuss it with your family.

Year A:
    Luke 24:13-35

Year B:
    Luke 24:35-48

Year C:
    John 21:1-19 or 21:1-14

Ministry

When we care for others, we minister to them. We take care of their needs and help them. Jesus asks us to do this. He asks us to serve one another.

During the Easter season we reflect on Jesus as a good shepherd. Jesus himself said, "I am the good shepherd" (John 10:14). He is a leader who serves others. Jesus is a shepherd who gave his life for his sheep.

The first Christians ministered to those in need. They were willing to serve others as Jesus taught them to do.

The Church grew and grew. Many of the new members needed help. So the apostles chose deacons. Stephen, a deacon, was one of the first followers of Jesus to die for his faith. He followed Jesus in ministering and in dying.

To Help You Remember

1. Describe what we mean when we say Jesus is a good shepherd.

2. How did the first Christians minister to those in need?

Sharing in Ministry

Create a diamanté-shaped poem by writing the following:

Line 2: two words that mean the same as "ministry"
Line 3: three "-ing" words about how you can minister to others
Line 4: four words naming skills and talents you have to give
Line 5: three ministering people in your parish
Line 6: two leaders in your parish

Ministry

_____ _____

_____ _____ _____

_____ _____ _____ _____

_____ _____ _____

_____ _____

Parish

Faith Focus

What does the Eucharist call us to share?

The Word of the Lord

Choose this year's gospel reading for the Fourth Sunday of Easter. Read and discuss it with your family.

Year A:
    John 10:1–10

Year B:
    John 10:11–18

Year C:
    John 10:27–30

What You See

The priest wears white vestments during the Easter season. White is a symbol of joy and life. We rejoice in Jesus' Resurrection.

We like to help others by sharing our talents. When we do that, we become self-giving people. We like to help others by giving them hope and laughter. When we do that, we become life-giving people.

Welcome to the Table

The Eucharist calls us to share our life with others. When we celebrate the Eucharist, we participate in the Paschal mystery. Together, we say or sing,
    "When we eat this bread and drink this cup, we proclaim your death, Lord Jesus, until you come in glory."

When the Church welcomes new members, they share in three sacraments. The Church washes them in the waters of Baptism. The Church anoints them with oil at Confirmation. The Church invites them to share the Eucharist.

To Help You Remember

1. What does the Eucharist call us to be?

2. What sacraments does the Church celebrate to welcome new members?

Eucharistic People

Read this rhyme about the celebration of the Eucharist. Then tell how you love and serve the Lord.

Each week on the Lord's Day,
We remember Jesus in a special way.

Many gather to sing and praise,
To hear and heed God's saving ways.

We celebrate together the great story,
How Jesus died and was raised to glory.

We share in his Body broken and Blood outpoured.
His gift is himself, our Savior and Lord.

It is the Lord we receive and the Lord we share.
We love and serve every day and everywhere.

This is how I will love and serve the Lord:

_____

_____ .

The Word of the Lord

Choose this year's gospel reading for the Fifth Sunday of Easter. Read and discuss it with your family.

Year A
John 14:1-12

Year B
John 15:1-8

Year C
John 13:31-35

Faith in Action

When someone is a good leader, we follow that person. We do what our leader does. Our actions show that we are good followers. As Christians we follow Jesus.

The apostle James says that our good words and works witness to Jesus' new life. James says that we show our faith in Jesus through our actions.

If we see someone without food or clothing, we must do something to help. James reminds us that we cannot just say, "Go in peace, keep warm, and eat well" (James 2:16). The apostle John says the same thing. "Children, let us love not in word or speech but in deed and truth" (1 John 3:18).

Today we are called to be witnesses to the good news of Jesus' Resurrection. God calls us to put our faith into action. The Holy Spirit helps us to do this.

To Help You Remember

1. What does the apostle James say we must do to witness to Jesus?

2. What are some ways you can put your faith into action?

Good News

Pretend you live in Our Town, USA. You are being interviewed about how Christians there carry out the work of Jesus. List some things you would tell the reporter.

_____

_____

_____

_____

_____

_____

_____

_____

_____

_____

Faith Focus

What did the followers of Jesus do to help the Church grow?

The Word of the Lord

Choose this year's gospel reading for the the Sixth Sunday of Easter. Read and discuss it with your family.

Year A
John 14:15-21

Year B
John 15:9-17

Year C
John 14:23-29

The Growing Church

When we do good, others want to do good too. When we do good, we become good news for others. That is what the followers of Jesus are. They are good news!

During the Masses of the Easter season, the first reading is from the Acts of the Apostles. We learn how the early Church grew under the guidance of the Holy Spirit.

The followers of Jesus welcomed others. They offered food and clothing and a warm place to live. They prayed for one another. They brought Jesus' healing to those who were sick and troubled.

Parish Holds Healing Mass

Family Donates Clothing to Hurricane Victims

3rd Grade Parents Sign Up for Neighborhood Watch

Share-A-Lunch Day Feeds Hundreds

Community Helps Flood Victims Clean Up Homes

Strangers saw this faith in action. They wanted to do good too. Followers of Jesus do more than talk about the good news of Jesus' Resurrection. They show that they are good news themselves! People see this. They want to follow Jesus too. The Church grows and grows.

Who's Who?

Find these passages in the Bible. Write down the name of the follower of Jesus.

I was chosen to take the place of Judas.

I am _____ .

Acts of the Apostles 1:24–26

I am a deacon. I gave my life for Christ.

I am _____ .

Acts of the Apostles 7: 54–60

Once I persecuted Christians.
Then I became an apostle and a missionary.

I am _____ .

Acts of the Apostles 9:1–8

My husband and I welcomed Paul to our home.
We are tentmakers.

I am _____ .

Acts of the Apostles 18:1–4

Faith Focus

What is the Good News that Christians share with others?

Stained-glass window of the Risen Christ.

The Word of the Lord

Choose this year's gospel reading for the Seventh Sunday of Easter. Read and discuss it with your family.

Year A
John 17:1-11

Year B
John 17:11-19

Year C
John 17:20-26

Proclaiming the Resurrection

We smile when we have good news. We share it with others. Our good news is that God has raised Jesus to new life. We share this good news by the way we live.

Before Jesus returned to his Father, he told his apostles to proclaim this good news to everyone. He told them to baptize and teach people. Jesus promised always to be with his followers.

After Jesus returned to his Father, the Holy Spirit came to his followers as Jesus promised. The Spirit guided and helped them. They lived joyful lives. They became generous and loving. Their actions showed others that they were a joyful, generous, and loving people.

To this day Jesus calls us to live in joyful hope. Our words and our actions proclaim the presence of the Risen Lord in our life.

To Help You Remember

1. What did the apostles do to proclaim the Good News?

2. How did the Holy Spirit help the apostles?

Love in Action

Use red to color in all the parts that show love in action.

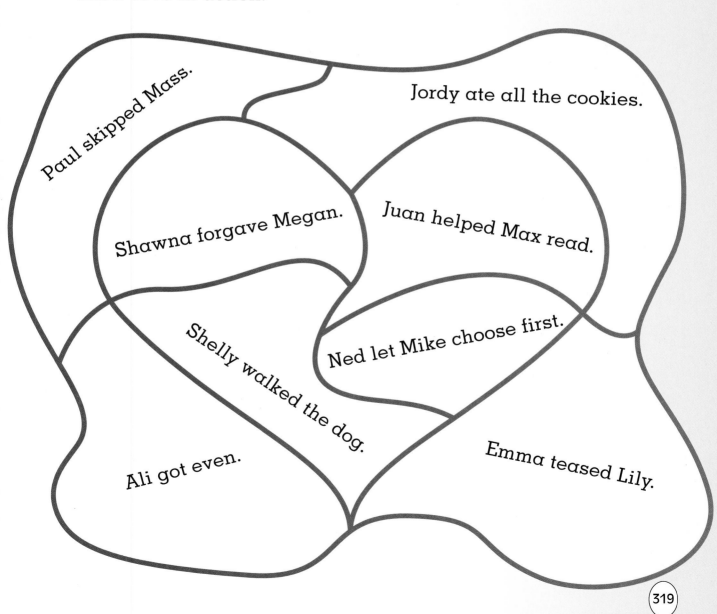

Paul skipped Mass.

Jordy ate all the cookies.

Shawna forgave Megan.

Juan helped Max read.

Shelly walked the dog.

Ned let Mike choose first.

Ali got even.

Emma teased Lily.

Pentecost

Faith Focus

How does the Holy Spirit help the Church to grow?

The Word of the Lord

Choose this year's gospel reading for Pentecost. Read and discuss it with your family.

Year A
  John 20:19-23

Year B
  John 20:19-23 or
  John 15:26-27, 16:12-15

Year C
  John 20:19-23 or
  John 14:15-16, 23-26

Pentecost

When we have difficult things to do, the Spirit helps us. We can depend on the Spirit. We can grow with the Spirit.

On Pentecost day the disciples were gathered in Jerusalem. As they prayed together, they heard the sound of a great wind. Flames gently settled over their heads.

Filled with the Holy Spirit, they boldly proclaimed the Risen Lord. Everyone understood their words!

Peter was full of courage. He stood in front of a huge crowd. He told them about Jesus' life, death, and Resurrection. He wanted everyone to know that the Risen Jesus was Messiah and Lord. Peter told the people to repent, be baptized, and receive the Holy Spirit.

Those who received the Holy Spirit grew into a great people who followed the Risen Lord. This great people is called the Church.

To Help You Remember

1. How does the Holy Spirit help us?

2. What did Peter tell the people after he received the Holy Spirit?

Come, Holy Spirit

LEADER: The spirit of the Lord shall rest upon him:

READER 1: a spirit of wisdom and of understanding,

READER 2: a spirit of counsel and of strength,

READER 3: a spirit of knowledge and of fear of the Lord. (Isaiah 11:2)

READER 4: I am David. When I was a young shepherd boy, Samuel anointed me with oil. The spirit of the Lord rushed upon me. (Based on 1 Samuel 16:12–13)

READER 5: I am Mary. The angel told me the Holy Spirit would come upon me. I would be Jesus' mother.
(Based on Luke 1:26–38)

READER 6: I am Jesus. I told the apostles: "I am sending the promise of my Father upon you; but stay in the city until you are clothed with power from on high." (Luke 24:49)

ALL: We are the Church. This is our prayer today: Come, Holy Spirit, fill the hearts of your faithful. Kindle in them the fire of your love.

From the Gospel Alleluia for Pentecost Sunday

Catholic Prayers and Practices

Sign of the Cross

In the name of the Father,
and of the Son,
and of the Holy Spirit. Amen.

Glory Prayer

Glory to the Father,
    and to the Son,
    and to the Holy Spirit:
as it was in the beginning, is now,
    and will be for ever. Amen.

Prayer to the Holy Spirit

Come, Holy Spirit, fill the hearts
    of your faithful.
And kindle in them the
    fire of your love.
Send forth your Spirit and
    they shall be created.
And you will renew the
    face of the earth.

Lord's Prayer

Our Father, who art in heaven,
hallowed be thy name;
Thy kingdom come;
Thy will be done on earth
    as it is in heaven.
Give us this day our daily bread;
and forgive us our trespasses
as we forgive those who trespass
    against us;
and lead us not into temptation,
but deliver us from evil.
Amen.

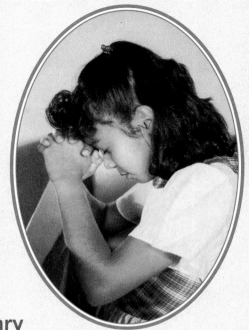

Hail Mary

Hail Mary, full of grace,
the Lord is with you!
Blessed are you among women,
and blessed is the fruit
    of your womb, Jesus.
Holy Mary, Mother of God,
pray for us sinners,
now and at the hour of our death.
Amen.

Act of Contrition

My God,
I am sorry for my sins
    with all my heart.
In choosing to do wrong
and failing to do good,
I have sinned against you
whom I should love above all things.
I firmly intend, with your help,
to do penance,
to sin no more,
and to avoid whatever leads me to
    sin.
Our Savior Jesus Christ
suffered and died for us.
In his name, my God, have mercy.

Apostles' Creed

I believe in God,
    the Father almighty,
    creator of heaven and earth.

I believe in Jesus Christ,
    his only Son, our Lord.
    He was conceived by the power
      of the Holy Spirit
      and born of the Virgin Mary.
    He suffered under Pontius Pilate,
      was crucified, died, and was
      buried.
    He descended to the dead.

On the third day he rose again.
    He ascended into heaven,
    and is seated at the right hand
      of the Father.
    He will come again to judge
      the living and the dead.

I believe in the Holy Spirit,
    the holy catholic Church,
    the communion of saints,
    the forgiveness of sins,
    the resurrection of the body,
    and the life everlasting. Amen.

Nicene Creed

We believe in one God,
    the Father, the Almighty,
    maker of heaven and earth,
    of all that is seen and unseen.

We believe in one Lord, Jesus Christ,
    the only Son of God,
    eternally begotten of the Father,
    God from God, Light from Light,
    true God from true God,
    begotten, not made, one in Being
      with the Father.
    Through him all things were
      made.
    For us men and for our salvation
      he came down from heaven:

by the power of the Holy Spirit
    he was born of the Virgin Mary,
    and became man.

For our sake he was crucified under
    Pontius Pilate;
    he suffered, died, and was buried.
    On the third day he rose again
    in fulfillment of the Scriptures;

he ascended into heaven
    and is seated at the right hand
    of the Father.
He will come again in glory to judge
    the living and the dead,
    and his kingdom will have no end.

We believe in the Holy Spirit, the
    Lord, the giver of life,
    who proceeds from the Father
    and the Son.
With the Father and the Son he is
    worshiped and glorified.
He has spoken through the
    Prophets.
We believe in one holy catholic
    and apostolic Church.
We acknowledge one baptism for
    the forgiveness of sins.
We look for the resurrection of the
    dead, and the life of the world
    to come.
    Amen.

Rosary

Catholics pray the rosary to honor Mary and remember the important events in the life of Jesus and Mary. There are fifteen mysteries of the rosary. The word *mystery* means "the wonderful things God has done for us."

We begin praying the rosary by praying the Apostles' Creed, the Lord's Prayer, and three Hail Marys. Each mystery of the rosary is prayed by praying the Lord's Prayer once, the Hail Mary ten times, and the Glory Prayer once. When we have finished the last mystery, we pray the Hail, Holy Queen.

Joyful Mysteries

1. The Annunciation
2. The Visitation
3. The Nativity
4. The Presentation
5. The Finding of Jesus in the Temple

Sorrowful Mysteries

6. The Agony in the Garden
7. The Scourging at the Pillar
8. The Crowning with Thorns
9. The Carrying of the Cross
10. The Crucifixion

Glorious Mysteries

11. The Resurrection
12. The Ascension
13. The Coming of the Holy Spirit
14. The Assumption of Mary
15. The Coronation of Mary

Hail, Holy Queen

Hail, holy Queen, mother of mercy,
hail, our life, our sweetness,
    and our hope.
To you we cry, the children of Eve;
to you we send up our sighs,
mourning and weeping
    in this land of exile.
Turn, then, most gracious advocate,
your eyes of mercy toward us;
lead us home at last
and show us the blessed fruit
    of your womb, Jesus:
O clement, O loving, O sweet
    Virgin Mary.

A Vocation Prayer

God, I know you will call me
for special work in my life.
Help me follow Jesus each day
and be ready to answer your call.

Grace Before Meals

Bless us, O Lord,
    and these your gifts
which we are about to receive
    from your goodness.
Through Christ our Lord.
Amen.

Grace After Meals

We give you thanks for all your gifts,
    almighty God,
living and reigning now and for ever.
Amen.

The Seven Sacraments

Sacraments of Initiation
    Baptism
    Confirmation
    Eucharist
Sacraments of Healing
    Reconciliation
    Anointing of the Sick
**Sacraments at the Service
 of Communion**
    Holy Orders
    Matrimony

The Great Commandment

"You shall love the Lord,
your God, with all your
heart, with all your soul,
and with all your mind.
You shall love your neighbor as
yourself."

MATTHEW 22:37, 39

The Ten Commandments

1. I am the LORD your God: you shall not have strange gods before me.
2. You shall not take the name of the LORD your God in vain.
3. Remember to keep holy the LORD's Day.
4. Honor your father and your mother.
5. You shall not kill.
6. You shall not commit adultery.
7. You shall not steal.
8. You shall not bear false witness against your neighbor.
9. You shall not covet your neighbor's wife.
10. You shall not covet your neighbor's goods.

The Beatitudes

"Blessed are the poor in spirit,
   for theirs is the kingdom of heaven.
Blessed are they who mourn,
   for they will be comforted.
Blessed are the meek,
   for they will inherit the land.
Blessed are they who hunger
      and thirst for righteousness,
   for they will be satisfied.
Blessed are the merciful,
   for they will be shown mercy.
Blessed are the clean of heart,
   for they will see God.
Blessed are the peacemakers,
   for they will be called children of God.
Blessed are they who are
      persecuted for the
      sake of righteousness,
   for theirs is the kingdom of heaven.
Blessed are you when they insult
      you and persecute you and utter
      every kind of evil against you
      [falsely] because of me.
   Rejoice and be glad, for your reward
      will be great in heaven."

MATTHEW 5:3–12

Corporal Works of Mercy

Feed people who are hungry.
Give drink to people who are thirsty.
Clothe people who need clothes.
Visit prisoners.
Shelter people who are homeless.
Visit people who are sick.
Bury people who have died.

Spiritual Works of Mercy

Help people who sin.
Teach people who are ignorant.
Give advice to people
   who have doubts.
Comfort people who suffer.
Be patient with other people.
Forgive people who hurt you.
Pray for people who are alive and for
   those who have died.

Precepts of the Church

1. Participate in Mass on Sundays and holy days of obligation.
2. Confess sins at least once a year.
3. Receive Holy Communion at least during the Easter season.
4. Keep holy Sunday and the holy days of obligation.
5. Observe the prescribed days of fasting and abstinence.
6. Provide for the material needs of the Church, according to one's abilities.

Stations of the Cross

1. Jesus is condemned to death.
2. Jesus accepts his cross.
3. Jesus falls the first time.
4. Jesus meets his mother.
5. Simon helps Jesus carry the cross.
6. Veronica wipes the face of Jesus.
7. Jesus falls the second time.
8. Jesus meets the women.
9. Jesus falls the third time.
10. Jesus is stripped of his clothes.
11. Jesus is nailed to the cross.
12. Jesus dies on the cross.
13. Jesus is taken down from the cross.
14. Jesus is buried in the tomb.
15. Jesus is raised from the dead.

The Sacrament of Reconciliation

Individual Rite of Reconciliation

Greeting
Scripture Reading
Confession of Sins
Act of Contrition
Absolution
Closing Prayer

Communal Rite of Reconciliation

Greeting
Scripture Reading
Homily
Examination of Conscience with Litany of Contrition and the Lord's Prayer
Individual Confession and Absolution
Closing Prayer

Celebrating Mass

Introductory Rites

Gathering
Entrance Procession and Hymn
Greeting
Penitential Rite
Gloria
Opening Prayer

Liturgy of the Word

First Reading (Usually from the
Old Testament)
Responsorial Psalm
Second Reading (Usually from
New Testament Letters)
Gospel Acclamation
Gospel
Homily
Creed (Profession of Faith)
General Intercessions

Liturgy of the Eucharist

Preparation of the Altar and Gifts
Eucharistic Prayer
Communion Rite
> Lord's Prayer
> Sign of Peace
> Breaking of Bread
> Communion

Concluding Rite

Greeting
Blessing
Dismissal

A

Abba
Abba is a word that means "father" in the language Jesus spoke. Jesus used this word when he prayed to God the Father. (page 238)

actual grace
Actual grace is the grace given to us by the Holy Spirit to help us follow Jesus. (page 224)

Advocate
Advocate is a name for the Holy Spirit that means "one who speaks for someone else." (page 74)

Ananias
Ananias was a follower of Jesus who lived in Damascus; through God's power he healed Saul's blindness. (page 102)

Annunciation
The announcement of Jesus' birth to Mary by the angel Gabriel is called the Annunciation. (page 30)

Apostles' Creed
The Apostles' Creed is one of the main creeds of the Catholic Church. (page 258)

Ascension
The return of the Risen Jesus to his Father is called the Ascension. (page 64)

B

Baptism
Baptism is the sacrament in which we are joined to Christ. Through Baptism we become members of the Church and followers of Jesus, our sins are forgiven, and we receive the gift of the Holy Spirit. (page 82)

Bethlehem
The town where Jesus was born is called Bethlehem. (page 34)

Blessed Sacrament
The Blessed Sacrament is the Eucharist that the Church keeps in the tabernacle to distribute to the sick and for private adoration. (page 166)

Body of Christ
Another name for the Church is the Body of Christ. (page 94)

C

Cana
Cana is a walled town about five miles from Nazareth where Jesus grew up. (page 154)

canticle
A song of praise to God is called a canticle. (page 32)

Christians
People who are baptized and believe in Jesus Christ are called Christians. (page 14)

Church
The Church is the People of God. (page 80)

communion of saints
The community of the followers of Jesus, both those living on earth and in heaven, is known as the communion of saints. (page 90)

Confirmation
One of the Sacraments of Initiation in which baptized people receive and celebrate the strengthening of the gift of the Spirit within them. (page 84)

contrition
Contrition is the sorrow we feel when we have done something wrong. (page 126)

conversion
The experience of changing one's heart and turning back to God is called conversion. (page 102)

covenant
The covenant is the solemn agreement between God and the Israelites. (page 184)

covet
Covet means "to want what someone else has." (page 208)

creation
All that God has made is known as creation. (page 20)

creed
A creed is a prayer that tells what we believe. (page 10)

crucified
To be crucified means to be put to death on a cross. (page 60)

Glossary

D

David
David was an ancestor of Jesus who was the second king of God's people. He wrote many of the psalms. (page 214)

disciples
The people who followed Jesus were called his disciples. (page 54)

Divine Providence
God's caring love is known as Divine Providence. (page 24)

E

Easter
Easter is the time of the year Christians celebrate and remember the Resurrection of Jesus. (page 62)

Easter Triduum
The Easter Triduum includes Holy Thursday, Good Friday, and the celebrations of the Easter Vigil and Easter Sunday. (page 174)

Eucharist
The Eucharist is the sacrament in which we receive the Body and Blood of Christ. The word *eucharist* means "to give thanks."(page 162)

F

faith
Belief and trust in God is called faith. Faith is both a gift from God that helps us to believe and trust in him and our response to that gift. (pages 30, 114)

feasts
Special days of the church year that are put aside to honor the saints are called feasts. (page 92)

forgive
To pardon someone for the wrong they have done is to forgive. (page 122)

G

Galilee
Galilee is a section of the land where Jesus lived and did the work God sent him to do while he was on earth. (page 154)

Genesis
The Book of Genesis is the first book of the Bible. (page 22)

Good Friday
Good Friday is the Friday before Easter Sunday. It is the day when we remember Jesus was crucified and died. (page 60)

Gospel
The Good News Jesus came to proclaim is called the Gospel. The first four books of the New Testament are known as the Gospels. (page 54)

Gospel according to John
The Gospel according to John is one of the first four books of the New Testament. The word *gospel* means "good news." (page 154)

grace
The gift of our sharing in the life of the Holy Trinity is called grace. (page 224)

Great Commandment
The Great Commandment is the commandment that all of God's laws depend on. It is, "You shall love God with all you heart, soul, and mind. You shall love others as you love yourself." (page 186)

H-I

Hail Mary
Hail Mary is a prayer based on the angel Gabriel's greeting to Mary at the Annunciation. (page 270)

heaven
Eternal life with God is called heaven. (page 226)

hell
A life separated from God forever after death is called hell. (page 228)

Holy Family
Jesus, Mary, and Joseph are known as the Holy Family. (page 52)

Holy Orders

Holy Orders is the sacrament that celebrates the ordaining of a man as a bishop, a priest, or a deacon to serve the People of God in the name of Jesus. (page 144)

Holy Spirit

The third Person of the Holy Trinity is the Holy Spirit. (page 72)

Holy Trinity

The Holy Trinity is the belief that there is one God in three Persons: God the Father, God the Son, God the Holy Spirit. (page 10)

honor

Honor means "to show respect and love for someone." (page 270)

humble

Humble means "being aware that God is the giver of all gifts and that we are all equal in God's sight." (page 136)

J

Jerusalem

The holiest city of the Jewish people is Jerusalem. (page 50)

Joseph

Joseph is the foster father of Jesus and the husband of Mary. (page 34)

judge

A judge was a leader of God's people before there were kings. (page 40)

K

kingdom of God

The time when people will live in peace and justice with God, one another, and all of God's creation is known as the kingdom of God. (page 54)

L

Last Supper

The Last Supper is the special meal that Jesus and his disciples ate together on the night before he died. (page 70)

Law of Moses

The Law of Moses was the Ten Commandments plus other important laws that guided the Jewish people. (page 100)

liturgical year

The seasons and feasts that make up the Church's year of worship is known as the liturgical year. (page 172)

liturgy

The liturgy is the Church's work of worshiping God. (page 172)

Liturgy of the Eucharist

The second part of the Mass, in which we remember and take part in Jesus' life, death, and Resurrection, is called the Liturgy of the Eucharist. (page 164)

Liturgy of the Word

The first part of the Mass, in which we listen and respond to God's word, is called the Liturgy of the Word. (page 164)

Lord's Prayer

The prayer that Jesus gave us is called the Lord's Prayer. (page 238)

M

Magnificat

Mary's canticle is called the Magnificat. (page 32)

Mary

Mary is the mother of Jesus, the Son of God who became like us. (page 30)

Mass

Mass is the celebration of listening to God's word and giving thanks and praise to God for the gift of Jesus. (page 164)

Matrimony

Matrimony is the sacrament that unites a baptized man and a baptized woman forever in love as husband and wife. (page 146)

Messiah

The word *Messiah* means "anointed one." We believe that Jesus is the anointed one promised by God. (page 50)

miracle
A miracle is a sign of God's power and presence with us. (page 156)

N

Nativity
The birth of Jesus is known as the Nativity. (page 34)

Nazareth
Nazareth was a small town in Galilee. (page 266)

New Testament
The second part of the Bible, which tells us about Jesus and the early Church, is called the New Testament. (page 12)

O

Old Testament
The first part of the Bible, which tells the story of God's people who lived before Jesus was born, is called the Old Testament. (page 12)

Ordinary Time
Ordinary Time includes the weeks of the liturgical year that are not the seasons of Advent, Christmas, Lent, or Easter. (page 176)

Our Father
Another name for the Lord's Prayer is the Our Father. (page 238)

P-Q

parable
A parable is a story that helped people understand and live what Jesus was teaching. (page 134)

Paschal mystery
The suffering, death, and Resurrection of Jesus is known as the Paschal mystery. (page 62)

patron saints
Saints who have been chosen to pray in a special way for people, countries, parishes, and for other reasons are called patron saints. (page 92)

Paul
Paul was the name that Saul took after he became a follower of Jesus. (page 102)

penance
A penance is a prayer or good deed that is given to us by the priest in the sacrament of Reconciliation. (page 126)

Pentecost
Pentecost is the day on which the Holy Spirit came upon the disciples of Jesus in Jerusalem. (page 72)

People of God
The People of God is a name we give to the Church. (page 14)

Persia
Persia is the ancient name of a country to the east of the Holy Land. (page 42)

Pharisee
A pharisee was one of a group of Jewish leaders who followed the Law of Moses as closely as possible. (page 100)

pray
To pray is to talk and listen to God. (page 236)

prayers of blessing
Prayers of blessing are prayers in which we remember that God is the Creator of everything good. (page 248)

prayers of intercession
Prayers of intercession are prayers in which we ask God to help others. (page 246)

prayers of petition
Prayers of petition are prayers in which we ask God to help us. (page 246)

prayers of praise
Prayers of praise are prayers in which we show our love and respect for God. (page 250)

prayers of thanksgiving
Prayers of thanksgiving are prayers in which we thank God for every blessing. (page 250)

private prayer
Private prayer is prayer a person prays alone. (page 240)

proclaim

To say aloud with the community is to proclaim. (page 258)

Psalms

Songs of prayer and praise to God found in the Bible are called psalms. The Book of Psalms is in the Old Testament. (page 24)

public prayer

Public prayer is prayer that people pray together. (page 240)

R

rabbi

The word *rabbi* means "teacher." (page 184)

Reconciliation

Reconciliation is the sacrament that celebrates God's forgiveness and mercy. This sacrament is also called the sacrament of Penance. (page 126)

respect

Respect means "to look up to," "to honor," or "to admire." (page 204)

Resurrection

God's raising Jesus from the dead to new life by the power of the Holy Spirit is called the Resurrection. (page 62)

S

sacraments

The seven special celebrations that make Jesus present to us in a special way and make us sharers in God's life and love are called sacraments. (page 112)

Sacraments at the Service of Communion

The sacraments of Matrimony and Holy Orders are known as the Sacraments at the Service of Communion. (page 144)

Sacraments of Initiation

The Sacraments of Initiation join us to Christ and welcome us into the church community. There are three Sacraments of Initiation. They are Baptism, Confirmation, and Eucharist. (page 82)

Sacred Scriptures

The Sacred Scriptures are the written word of God. The Sacred Scriptures are also called the Bible. (page 12)

saints

The saints are people whose love for God is stronger than anything else. The Church honors some people who have died by naming them saints. (page 90)

sanctifying grace

Sanctifying grace is the grace we receive at Baptism. It makes us holy. It makes us like God. (page 224)

sin

Freely choosing to do or say something that we know is against God's Law is called sin. (page 124)

Stephen

Stephen was the first Christian who died for his faith. (page 100)

stewards

People who have the responsibility to care for the things they have been given are called stewards. (page 218)

T-U

tabernacle

A tabernacle is a special box in which the Blessed Sacrament is kept. (page 166)

Ten Commandments

The Ten Commandments are the laws given by God to Moses on Mount Sinai. The Ten Commandments help us to love God, others, and ourselves. (page 194)

Temple

The Temple is the holy place in Jerusalem where the Jewish people worshiped God. (page 50)

V-Z

Visitation

The visit Mary, the mother of Jesus, had with Elizabeth, her relative, is called the Visitation. (page 32)

vocation

Our call from God to share in Jesus' life and work is called our vocation. We live this call in many ways. (page 142)

Index

Cover: Carol-Anne Wilson

PHOTO CREDITS:

Abbreviated as follows: (bkgd) background; (t) top; (b) bottom; (l) left; (r) right; (c) center.

Chapter 1: Page 7 (t,l), © Donald F. Wristen/RCL; 7 (t,r), © 2000 The Crosiers/Gene Plaisted, OSC; 7 (b), © Joseph Van Os/The Image Bank/PNI; 9, 12, 16 (t),© 2000 The Crosiers/Gene Plaisted, OSC; 16 (c), © SuperStock/Pinacoteca di Brera, Milan, Italy; 16 (b), © Don Rutledge/The Picture Cube, Inc.

Chapter 2: Page 19, © Joseph Van Os/The Image Bank/PNI; 20 (t,l), © Charles Krebs/All Stock/PNI; 20 (t,r), © Bruce Hands/Stock, Boston/PNI; 20 (c), © William Johnson/Stock, Boston/PNI; 20 (b), © 1997 Photo Disc, Inc.; 21, © Skip Moody/Rainbow/PNI; 22 (l), © David Hiser/Tony Stone Images; 22 (t,r), © David Young-Wolff/Photo Edit/PNI; 22 (b,r), © Peter Cade/Tony Stone Images; 26 (t), © 2000 The Crosiers/Gene Plaisted, OSC; 26 (b), © Matt Ristow.

Chapter 3: Page 29, © Tony Freeman/Photo Edit; 30,34, © 2000 The Crosiers/Gene Plaisted, OSC; 36 (t), © SuperStock, Inc.; 36 (c), © Bill Wittman; 36 (b,l & r), © 2000 The Crosiers/Gene Plaisted, OSC.

Chapter 4: Page 39, © 2000 The Crosiers/Gene Plaisted, OSC; 44 (l), © Alan Oddie/Photo Edit; 44 (r), © Bob Daemmrich/Stock, Boston/PNI; 45, © Pedro Meyer/Black Star/PNI; 46, © Rich Friedman/Black Star/PNI.

Chapter 5: Page 49, © Anne Hamersky; 52 (all), © 2000 The Crosiers/Gene Plaisted, OSC; 56, © David Young-Wolff/Photo Edit/PNI.

Chapter 6: Page 59, © Donald F. Wristen/RCL; 60, © Bill Wittman; 66 (all), © 2000 The Crosiers/Gene Plaisted, OSC.

Chapter 7: Page 69, © 2000 The Crosiers/Gene Plaisted, OSC.

Chapter 8: Page 79, © Michael Freeman/Bruce Coleman/PNI; 82 (all), 83, courtesy of Jeff Nicklas, Todd Jaranowski, David Franck; 84, © 2000 The Crosiers/Gene Plaisted, OSC; 84-85 (bkgd), © Photo Disc, Inc.; 85, © 2000 The Crosiers/Gene Plaisted, OSC; 86, © Jeff Greenberg/Photo Edit.

Chapter 9: Page 89, © SuperStock, Inc.; 92 (bkgd), 93(bkgd), © Corbis/Digital Stock; 94 (t), © Myrleen Ferguson/Photo Edit; 94 (b), © SuperStock, Inc.; 96, © 2000 The Crosiers/Gene Plaisted, OSC.

Chapter 10: Page 99, © 2000 The Crosiers/Gene Plaisted, OSC; 106 (bkgd), © Wood River Gallery/PNI; 106, © Redemptorist Provincial Archives.

Chapter 11: Page 109 (t,l), © 2000 The Crosiers/Gene Plaisted, OSC; 109 (t,r), © Photo Disc, Inc.; 109 (b), © Myrleen Ferguson/Photo Edit; 111, © 2000 The Crosiers/Gene Plaisted, OSC; 112 (t,l & b), © 2000 The Crosiers/Gene Plaisted, OSC; 112 (r), Stephen McBrady/Photo Edit; 113 (t,l), © Michael Newman/Photo Edit; 113 (l,c), © Bill Wittman; 113 (b,l), © 2000 The Crosiers/Gene Plaisted, OSC; 113 (r), Myrleen Ferguson Cate/Photo Edit; 116 (t), © John Feingersh/Stock, Boston/PNI; 116 (b), © Myrleen Ferguson Cate/Photo Network/PNI; 117 (t), © Derek Cole/Southern Stock/PNI; 117 (b), © Alan Oddie/Photo Edit; 118 (l & c,r), © Bill Wittman; 118 (c,l & b,r), © 1997 Artville, LLC.; 118 (b,c), © Dennis Full/RCL; 118 (t,r), © 2000 The Crosiers/Gene Plaisted, OSC.

Chapter 12: Page 121, © Myrleen Ferguson/Photo Edit/PNI; 122 © 2000 The Crosiers/Gene Plaisted, OSC; 124 (t), © Laura Dwight/Photo Edit; 124 (b), © Stewart Cohen/Tony Stone Images; 125, © Brian Syntyk/Masterfile; 126, © Myrleen Ferguson/Photo Edit; 128, © Gamma Liaison.

Chapter 13: Page 131, © 2000 The Crosiers/Gene Plaisted, OSC; 132, © Karl Holtsnider; 136, © Bill Wittman.

Chapter 14: Page 141, © SuperStock, Inc.; 144 (t), © Donald F. Wristen/RCL; 144 (b), © 2000 The Crosiers/Gene Plaisted, OSC; 146 (t), © Spencer Grant/FPG International; 146 (b), © Charles Gupton/Allstock/PNI; 148, © Monkmeyer/Smith.

Chapter 15: Page 151, © 2000 The Crosiers/Gene Plaisted, OSC; 158 (t), © James A. Sugar/Black Star/PNI; 158 (c,b), © Bill Wittman.

Chapter 16: Page 161, © 2000 The Crosiers/Gene Plaisted, OSC; 164, © Cleo/Photo Edit; 165, 166, © Donald F. Wristen/RCL; 168, © Myrleen Ferguson/Photo Edit.

Chapter 17: Page 171, © Photo Disc, Inc.; 172 (all), © 2000 The Crosiers/Gene Plaisted, OSC; 173 (t), © Martha McBride/Unicorn Stock Photos; 173 (b), © 2000 The Crosiers/Gene Plaisted, OSC; 174, 175, © Bill Wittman.

Chapter 18: Page 181 (t,l), © 2000 The Crosiers/Gene Plaisted, OSC; 181 (t,r), © Index Stock Photography; 181 (b), © Viesti Associates, Inc.; 183, © James L. Shaffer; 184 (t), © David Young-Wolff/Photo Edit/PNI; 184 (b), © Lori Adamski Peek/Tony Stone Images; 188 (t,l), © Lawrence Migdale/Stock, Boston/PNI; 188 (t,r), © John Lei/Stock, Boston/PNI; 188 (b,l), © Tony Freeman/Photo Edit/PNI; 188 (b,r), © Robert Brenner/Photo Edit; 190 (t), © Dennis MacDonald/Photo Edit; 190 (b), © Myrleen Ferguson Cate/Photo Network/PNI.

Chapter 19: Page 193, 194 (b), © 2000 The Crosiers/Gene Plaisted, OSC; 194-195 (bkgd), © Uniphoto; 196 (t), © Lori Adamski Peek/Tony Stone Images; 196 (b), © James L. Shaffer; 198 (t), © Lori Adamski Peek/Tony Stone Images; 198 (b), © Richard Hutchings/Photo Edit/PNI.

Chapter 20: Page 203, © Index Stock Photography; 206 (t), © Dean Berry/Liaison International; 206 (b), © David Hanover/Tony Stone Images; 207, © David Young-Wolff/Photo Edit/PNI; 208 (t), © Karl Weatherly/All Stock/PNI; 208 (b), © Tom McCarthy/Photo Edit; 209, © Tony Freeman/Photo Edit/PNI; 210, © Donald F. Wristen/RCL.

Chapter 21: Page 213, © Viesti Associates, Inc.; 216 (t), © Jose Azel/Aurora/PNI; 216 (c), © Randy Wells/All Stock/PNI; 216 (b), © Darrell Gulin/Tony Stone Images; 217, © J. Sneesby/B. Wilkins/Tony Stone Images; 218, © SuperStock, Inc.; 220-221 (bkgd), © SuperStock, Inc.

Chapter 22: Page 223, © Novastock/Stock Connection/PNI; 224, © Bill Wittman; 226, © Joanna B. Pinneo/Aurora/PNI; 230, © Bill Wittman.

Chapter 23: Page 233 (t,l), © Matt Ristow; 233 (t,r), © 2000 The Crosiers/Gene Plaisted, OSC; 233 (b), 235, © Jeff Greenberg/Photo Edit/PNI; 236, © 2000 The Crosiers/Gene Plaisted, OSC; 238, © Bill Wittman; 240 (t), © Karim Shamsi-Basha; 240 (b), © Bill Wittman; 242 (t & c,r), © Sam Martinez/RCL; 242 (c,l), © Matt Ristow; 242 (b), © Anthony Jambor.

Chapter 24: Page 245, © Jeff Greenberg/Stock, Boston/PNI; 246 (t), © John Troha/Black Star/PNI; 246 (b), © Chris Harris/Stock South/PNI; 247 (t), © Bob Daemmrich/Stock, Boston/PNI; 247 (b), © David Young-Wolff/Photo Edit/PNI; 248, © Donald F. Wristen/RCL; 252 (t), © Donald F. Wristen; 252 (c), © Robert Cushman Hayes; 252 (b), © Bill Wittman.

Chapter 25: Page 255, © Matt Ristow; 256, © 2000 The Crosiers/Gene Plaisted, OSC; 259, © Photo Disc, Inc.; 260, © 2000 The Crosiers/Gene Plaisted, OSC.

Chapter 26: Page 265, 268, © 2000 The Crosiers/Gene Plaisted, OSC; 272 (t), © Bill Wittman; 272 (b), © Matt Ristow.

Liturgical Seasons: Page 275 (t,l), © 2000 The Crosiers/Gene Plaisted, OSC; 275 (t,r), © Michael Newman/Photo Edit; 275 (b), © Myrleen Ferguson/Photo Edit; 276, © Donald F. Wristen/RCL; 278, © Bill and Peggy Wittman; 284, 286, © 2000 The Crosiers/Gene Plaisted, OSC; 290, © Myrleen Ferguson/Photo Edit; 292 (l), © Kindra Clinett/The Picture Cube, Inc.; 292 (r), © Tony Freeman/Photo Edit; 294 (t), © Myrleen Ferguson/Photo Edit; 294 (b), © Bob Thomas/Tony Stone Images; 296, © Tony Freeman/Photo Edit/PNI; 298, © 2000 The Crosiers/Gene Plaisted, OSC; 300, © Bill Wittman; 302, 304, © 2000 The Crosiers/Gene Plaisted, OSC; 306, © Corbis/Digital Stock; 310 (t), © Myrleen Ferguson Cate/Photo Edit; 310 (b), © Charles Thatcher/Tony Stone Images; 312, © Michael Newman/Photo Edit; 314 (t), © Andy Sacks/Tony Stone Images; 314 (b), © Bob Torrez/Tony Stone Images; 318, © Corbis/Digital Stock; 320, © 2000 The Crosiers/Gene Plaisted, OSC; 322, © Myrleen Ferguson/Photo Edit; 324, © Monkmeyer/Sheridan; 325, © Frank Siteman/Tony Stone Images; 326, © Myrleen Ferguson/Photo Edit/PNI; 327, © Donald F. Wristen/RCL; 328 (t), © 2000 The Crosiers/Gene Plaisted, OSC; 328 (b), © Donald F. Wristen/RCL.

ART CREDITS:

Chapter 1: Page 10, 11, Karen Malzeke-McDonald; 13, Desktop Miracles; 14, Mari Goering; 15, 17, Karen Malzeke-McDonald.

Chapter 2: Page 23, Karen Malzeke-McDonald; 24, Gary Torrisi.

Chapter 3: Page 32, Margaret Sanfilippo; 33, Desktop Miracles; 35, Karen Malzeke-McDonald; 37, Desktop Miracles.

Chapter 4: Page 40 (all), 41 (t), Mari Goering; 41 (b), Dynamic Graphics, Inc.; 42, Mari Goering; 43, 45, Desktop Miracles.

Chapter 5: Page 50, 51, Deborah White; 53, Karen Malzeke-McDonald; 54, Gary Torrisi; 55, Desktop Miracles.

Chapter 6: Page 62, Mari Goering; 63, Desktop Miracles; 64, Gary Torrisi; 65, Karen Malzeke-McDonald.

Chapter 7: Page 70, Bob Niles; 72, Deborah White; 73, 76, Karen Malzeke-McDonald.

Chapter 8: Page 80, Mari Goering; 83, Linda Yakel.

Chapter 9: Page 90, 91, L. S. Pierce; 93; Desktop Miracles.

Chapter 10: Page 100, 102, 104, Lane Gregory.

Chapter 11: Page 114, Gary Torrisi; 115, Karen Malzeke-McDonald; 119, Desktop Miracles.

Chapter 13: Page 133, 134, Mari Goering; 137, Jerry Hopkins; 138, Karen Malzeke-McDonald.

Chapter 14: Page 142, Gary Torrisi.

Chapter 15: Page 152, Yoshi Miyake; 154, 155, John Martin; 156 (all), 157, Bob Niles.

Chapter 16: Page 162, Gary Torrisi; 163, Desktop Miracles.

Chapter 17: Page 176 (t & b,l), Pamela Johnson; 176 (b,r), Dick Smolinski.

Chapter 18: Page 186, Gary Torrisi, 191, Victor Harper.

Chapter 19: Page 195, Karen Malzeke-McDonald.

Chapter 20: Page 204, Lokken Millis; 205, Karen Malzeke-McDonald; 211, Barbara Combs Marks.

Chapter 21: Page 214, Lane Gregory; 215, Karen Malzeke-McDonald.

Chapter 22: Page 225, Debi Seiler; 227, Desktop Miracles; 228, Lane Gregory; 231, Desktop Miracles.

Chapter 23: Page 241, L.S. Pierce; 243, Debi Seiler.

Chapter 24: Page 250, Gary Torrisi.

Chapter 25: Page 261, Desktop Miracles; 262, Karen Malzeke-McDonald.

Chapter 26: Page 266 (all), 267, Doris Ettlinger; 269, Jerry Hopkins; 270, Karen Malzeke-McDonald.

Liturgical Seasons: Page 277, 279, Jerry Hopkins; 280, Yoshi Miyake; 282, Jan Palmer; 288, Margaret Sanfilippo; 289, Dynamic Graphics, Inc.; 295, Victor Harper; 297, Deborah White; 299, Auto/FX Corporation; 301, Victor Harper; 307, Cory Davis/Victoria Barth; 308, Debra McClatchey-Ames; 313, 317, Cory Davis.